"This is the book I have been waiting for! *Living in a Gray World* approaches the issue of homosexuality biblically and yet with tremendous compassion and care. I wish every teen would read it."

SEAN MCDOWELL
Professor at Biola University
and the author of fifteen books, including
Ethix: Being Bold in a Whatever World

"This book is hands-down the best resource I've seen on this subject for Christian young people—biblical, grace-soaked, and incredibly practical. So many Christian teens (and their parents!) are confused about, scared of, and yet immersed in a culture where formerly black-and-white lines about sexuality have blurred gray. But rather than fear, judge, or ignore this shift, Preston guides us through Scripture to not only help us see God's best plan for sexuality but, perhaps even more importantly, remind us that we're talking about individual people with unique stories—not just discussing an 'issue.' I cannot recommend this book more!"

JESSIE MINASSIAN
Resident "big sis" at LifeLoveandGod.com,
and author of *Crushed, Unashamed,*
and *Backwards Beauty*

Other books by the author

People to Be Loved

LIVING IN A GRAY WORLD

A Christian Teen's Guide to Understanding Homosexuality

PRESTON SPRINKLE

NEW YORK TIMES BESTSELLING AUTHOR

ZONDERVAN

Living in a Gray World
Copyright © 2015 by Preston Sprinkle

This title is also available as a Zondervan ebook. Visit www.zondervan.com/ebooks.

Requests for information should be addressed to:
Zondervan, 3900 Sparks Dr. SE, Grand Rapids, Michigan 49546

ISBN 978-0-310-75206-6

Published in association with the literary agency of Wolgemuth & Associates, Inc.

Cover design: Brand Navigation
Interior design: Denise Froehlich

Printed in the United States of America

HB 03.05.2024

ACKNOWLEDGMENTS

I want to thank the many parents, teens, youth pastors, and college students who encouraged me to write this book and who read previous drafts of it. In particular, Jesse Minassian first alerted me to the need for this type of book, and read through its first draft and offered many helpful comments. Thanks also to Bert Alcorn, Mattie Dodson, McKensey Wise, and Pam Wollam for reading over earlier drafts. Your incisive comments regarding readability and tone were invaluable. A special thanks to Dr. Mark Yarhouse for reading through chapter 4 and offering much-needed critical feedback. And thanks—as always—to my wife, Christine, and my four children, Kaylea, Aubrey, Josie, and Cody, for your constant love and encouragement.

My heart goes out to the thousands of teens and students who are wrestling with their faith and sexuality—oftentimes with no one to talk to. My hope and prayer are that this book will not only help you in your journey, but encourage others to journey with you.

TABLE OF CONTENTS

A MESSAGE TO PARENTS

This book is written primarily for students between the ages of fifteen and twenty-two. Many parents therefore will wonder if their sons and daughters should read this book. So let me introduce myself and tell you what this book is all about.

I'm a husband to my beautiful and energetic wife, Christine, and father of four children. I've also been a college professor since 2008 and have a huge heart for the next generation of Christians. I received a PhD in New Testament and Ancient Judaism from Aberdeen University (Scotland) and have written several books about the Bible and theology. As a professor, I spend a lot of time with college students, and I sometimes speak to high school students as well. As a result, I've developed a strong understanding of the questions and issues they're wrestling with. And over the last few years, the topic of homosexuality is usually at the top of the list. Their questions have caused me to spend a considerable amount of time studying the topic as thoroughly as I can. I believe—and most people would agree—that the question of homosexuality is one of the most important ethical questions facing the church today. One of the problems I've encountered is that high school and college students are getting bombarded with opinions about homosexuality from the media, school, friends, and coworkers, but the church often stays silent. Maybe you've talked to them about the topic, or maybe you haven't. My guess, though, is that even if you have, your voice is only one of many perspectives that are shaping their thinking on the issue. Hence, the reason for this book.

Let me tell you up front where I stand on the question of homosexuality. I believe that the Bible prohibits homosexual behavior. I don't believe this just because I've been told to, nor do I believe it because of my Christian upbringing. I believe this because after studying the topic for a few years, I've discovered that the so-called traditional view is correct. The Bible only endorses opposite-sex marriages and prohibits same-sex sexual relations. However, I also believe that Christians have not always reflected the love of Christ in the ways they've dealt with the issue of homosexuality. And many gay and lesbian people have been greatly hurt by the church's unloving and judgmental posture. We need to be truthful, but we also need to be loving. We shouldn't sacrifice the truth for the sake of love, or stop loving in order to be truthful. Jesus exemplifies both truth and love; therefore, so should we. And that's what this book is all about. How to be truthfully loving and lovingly truthful.

A few years ago, a friend of mine, who has a ministry with teen girls, told me that she gets questions about homosexuality almost daily. She's looked for some sort of resource to give these students but hasn't found any. Knowing that I've been studying the topic, she encouraged me to write a book for students. I also saw the need for this book, and the rest is history.

You probably want to know what I'm going to talk about in this book. As a parent, I know I would! So let me give you a quick snapshot. In the following pages, I'm going to have a very frank conversation with my student readers about homosexuality. I'm going to wrestle with hard questions and do my best to give biblical answers. As a parent, this might make you nervous; I don't know. You may wonder what I'm going to say—especially with such a debated topic as homosexuality. So let me give you a sneak peek into the three themes I'm going to cover in this book.

First, I'm going to educate my readers about homosexuality and other related issues, such as what it means to identify as transgender and intersex. Before we give an answer to a question, we must fully understand the question! The same is true of homosexuality. We need to understand all the different questions being raised before we provide biblical answers to those questions. So in this book, I'm going to explain the various concepts and terms that surround this discussion. I'm also going to share a lot of personal testimonies from people who are gay. After all, hearing the stories of real people is often the best way to become educated about homosexuality.

Second, I'm going to explain what the Bible says about homosexuality. I do this most explicitly in chapters 2–3 and in the appendix. Again, I do believe that same-sex sexual relations are sin. However, I also believe that Christians have historically done a very poor job of loving and pastoring people who are gay. So there's a healthy tension of truth and love woven throughout this book. It's a tension our students need to wrestle with. It's a tension that *we* need to wrestle with.

Third, I'm going to cultivate a heart for people. As I often say, homosexuality is not about some issue to debate; it's about people to love—people, like you and me, who need Jesus. On that note, if you have a son or daughter who is either gay or wrestling with same-sex attraction, this book will be good for both of you to read. I'm not just writing this book to straight students, but to all students. In fact, chapter 6 is written directly to students who experience same-sex attraction.

I hope and pray that this book will help guide your sons and daughters in thinking more biblically and compassionately about this important topic. And if the topic of homosexuality is something you want to learn more about, then you might want to read my other book, *People to Be Loved*. It's almost twice as long as this book and deals with the Bible and homosexuality in much more depth.

CHAPTER ONE

A CONVERSATION ABOUT HOMOSEXUALITY

His hands were trembling and his face dripped with sweat. He didn't want to go in there, but knew he had to.

My friend Jordan was anxiously waiting in his car outside the church office.[1] He had recently come to grips with the fact that he was attracted to guys, and he'd even mustered up the courage to tell his pastor. But now he was about to go into a room full of church leaders and tell them, "I . . . I am . . . I'm. Gay. I'm gay." He could hardly say the words out loud in the safety of his car. But he knew he had to go. He had to tell them.

Jordan was helping out in the youth group at church and had just completed a year of college. He had spent several years wrestling with his same-sex attraction, though his commitment to the Bible prevented him from acting on it. He hadn't even touched another guy romantically. But no one at this church had known about his struggle.

When he entered the room, he was greeted with smiles. With palms still dripping with sweat, he decided to get it

---

1   "Jordan" is a pseudonym for my friend. The following story represents the basic gist of what happened, though some phrases and scenes come from other events in Jordan's life.

over with. "I know you all trust me and allow me to help out in church. So, I wanted to let you know that . . . I mean . . . I want to confess that, well . . . I'm sort of . . . I'm . . . I struggle with same-sex attraction. I'm . . . I'm attracted to guys."

Silence.

"I thought he was a Christian?" one leader said to another, forgetting that Jordan was still in the room. A few feet away. With ears. That worked.

"Jordan, when did you decide this?"

"Um . . . when? What do you mean? I . . . . I didn't decide this. I don't *want* to be attracted to guys."

The leader continued, "You know, Jordan, what God thinks about homosexuals? The Bible says that they are an abomination!"

Jordan was taken aback. He didn't know what to say. The line between homosexual *practice* and struggling with same-sex *attraction* was painfully blurred. And the confusion continued to dehumanize Jordan limb by limb.

"Jordan, we can't condone someone with your lifestyle," another leader interjected with polished conviction.

Lifestyle? Jordan thought. *I haven't even touched another person. I'm probably more pure than any other guy my age. Lifestyle?!*

Before Jordan could respond, another leader added, "And what about our children? I mean, we can't have you working with our children!"

Jordan didn't know how to respond. "Um . . . sir, I . . . I'm not a *pedophile*. I don't struggle with wanting to have sex with children."

As Jordan sat through the rest of the rather brief meeting, he felt his humanity slipping away. He might as well have been stuffed in a cage and sold to the zoo. The last thing Jordan remembers that night is heading to his car, locking the door, squeezing the steering wheel until his fingers turned white, and screaming away his pain.

Ugh.

My heart breaks whenever I think about Jordan in that church office. Over the years I've talked with a lot of gay and lesbian people. Almost all of them have similar stories of feeling less than human and being painfully misunderstood. If there's one thing I've learned, it's that we've got to put flesh on this topic. We've got to stop talking about issues and start talking about human beings. As Jordan's story shows, focusing on truth with little compassion can actually damage other people who are made in God's image.

LET'S HAVE A CONVERSATION

I think it's time to have a conversation about homosexuality. No, not a feisty, angry, explosive conversation—maybe you've had some of those before. Let's have a cordial conversation. An honest talk filled with authenticity and love. One where hard questions are raised and genuine answers are given. And if there is no clear answer, a simple "Let's keep thinking about that" will do just fine.

I know it sounds weird for a book to be a "conversation"—especially since you won't be able to talk back at this book without others thinking you're nuts. But I think this book can still be a discussion. I'm not going to lecture at you, cram info down your throat, or even tell you what you must believe. I'm going to converse with you through these pages as if we're hanging out at a coffee shop together. I'll bring up the same subjects you're probably wondering about, and I'll try to raise some pushbacks that you might have.

So let's have an honest dialogue about a very tough topic. I'm sure you have questions. Good questions, hard questions, weird questions, or questions you can't ask anyone else. For instance:

Can I be friends with someone who's gay?

How should I respond when my sister tells me she's a lesbian?

Should I attend a gay wedding?

If two people love each other and they're not hurting anyone else, then can't they get married?

Does the Bible really say homosexuality is wrong?

If people are born gay, then doesn't this mean God made them that way?

And . . . are people born gay?

I feel like I'm attracted to the same sex, but I have no one to talk to. What should I do?

I'm glad you asked these good questions. There are no bad questions in our conversation. (There could be some bad answers out there, but no bad questions.) Now let me be up front. I'm not going to pretend that there's one cookie-cutter answer to every question. There's not. Some questions have simple answers, but many don't. Most questions require a lot of thought and honest discussion. So let's have that discussion.

REAL PEOPLE

Let's begin our conversation by meeting some real people. Real people with real stories. My hope is that hearing their stories will help us "put flesh" on the topic of homosexuality.

The first friend I want to introduce to you is Dan. Dan is a gay man happily married to another man. Dan isn't very religious and he often gets frustrated with conservative Christians. He mocks them, yells at them, and would love to see the conservative church simply fade out of existence. Dan is the type of guy many Christians think of when they hear the word *homosexuality*. A feisty, angry, church-hating loudmouth who loves to fire off mean comments on blogs and Twitter.

And then there's Maddie. Maddie is a lesbian, but she's not attracted to women. This seems weird until you hear her story. When Maddie was nine years old, her dad chained her to a toilet in the basement and fed her scraps of food for three months. He then apologized, released her, and warned her that he'd kill her if she told anyone about what had happened. As if that wasn't bad enough, he raped her over the next four years. And that's why Maddie is a lesbian. She isn't attracted to women, but she chooses to be a lesbian because she vows that because of what her father did, "no man will ever touch me again."

Unlike Maddie, Justin was raised in a healthy Christian home and became a follower of Christ at a young age. His mom wasn't domineering, his dad was around, his sisters didn't dress him up in pink, and he wasn't sexually abused. Justin breaks all the stereotypes of what some people say "makes" people gay. Justin is a Bible-believing Christian who grew up in a loving family. But when Justin was fourteen, he realized he was attracted to the same sex. He then spent several years studying what the Bible says about same-sex relations, and he ended up concluding that, based on his interpretation, the Bible does not condemn consensual, loving, same-sex marriages.

You've already met my friend Jordan. He grew up a lot like Justin, but Jordan believes that acting on homosexual desires is a sin. Jordan is still attracted to guys, but he's committed to a life without marriage and sex because he's convinced that same-sex relations are wrong and that he can best serve God through celibacy. In case you're wondering, Jordan got through that frightful evening with the leaders at his church. He ended up forgiving all of them for making him feel less than human. And today, he actually has a very good relationship with people at his church. Jordan is one of the most amazing Christians I've ever met. In fact, he's one of the most life-giving humans I've ever hung out with.

My friend Lesli is a female, but from the time she was four years old she believed that she was a boy. Biologically, Lesli is female. But psychologically and mentally, she identified as a male. In other words, she realized that she was "transgender" (we'll get to that word later). She didn't choose to feel this way. But now Lesli is a believer in Christ and helps other transgender men and women work through what it means to experience gender confusion.

The last person I want you to meet is Eric. He too was born into a Christian home and discovered he was attracted to the same sex at fourteen. Throughout high school, Eric was mocked, beat up, and made to feel less than human by Christians and non-Christians. When he came out to his parents about being gay, they told him he was an abomination and kicked him out of the house. A year later, he committed suicide. Eric died lonely, confused, and unloved.

Each one of these people has some experience with homosexuality. But as you can see, their stories are as different as night and day. They all have a unique set of experiences, joys and fears, things they hate and love, things that make them smile and other things that make them crazy mad. And they have stories. Lots and lots of stories. Stories that make them sing, and stories that make them shudder with cold sweat. I've introduced you to Dan, Maddie, Justin, Jordan, Lesli, and Eric because there's something we really need to agree on up front. What I'm about to say will be *foundational* to everything I write in this book. However you feel about homosexuality, the Bible, or whatever, this truth is *nonnegotiable*:

Homosexuality is about *people* and not about some *issue*.

We're talking about people. People who have been raped into lesbianism, and people who have been born with same-sex attraction. (We'll get into the whole "born with it" debate later as well.) Men who feel more like women, and women who feel like men. Some gay and lesbians who act on their attraction, and others who don't. Some who believe in Jesus, and others who despise the Christian faith. And those who used to love Jesus but were so mocked and hated by Christians that they've left the church. Or committed suicide. The point is, there's no one-size-fits-all category for gay and lesbian people. Just like you and me and everybody else, they're different. So whether you are gay or straight or somewhere in between, you have a unique story. We are all individual human beings. And this book—I mean, *conversation*—is about understanding fellow human beings.

Throughout our conversation, you and I are going to ask some hard questions and sort through some tough debates. We're going to look at the Bible, psychology, and philosophy. And we're going to listen to a lot of stories. As we wrestle with all of this, never forget that we're talking about people—real people with real feelings.

LGBTQTIAP

Before we really dive into our conversation, we need to get on the same page about some important words. One thing

I've learned from talking to gay people over the years is that words really matter, *especially* in this discussion. There's a stupid saying that I used to hear as a kid. Maybe you've heard it too. It goes like this: "Sticks and stones will break my bones but words will never hurt me." This is terribly wrong. Yes, a big old stone will probably break your bones, but words have the power to crush your heart. Millions of people have been psychologically and emotionally slaughtered over something they were called more than twenty years ago. Eating disorders, depression, and suicide are often caused by hurtful words. Words have the power to hurt and to heal, to build up and to tear down. And unfortunately, many gay and lesbian individuals have been slashed by words that feel like razor blades across their eyeballs.

Take the word *lifestyle*. Too often, the terms *gay* or *homosexual* are quickly followed by the word *lifestyle*, like in Jordan's conversation with his church leaders. We need to be careful with this term. Lifestyle. Does every gay person have the same *lifestyle*?

Think about it. How would you feel if someone talked about the "straight lifestyle" and then lumped you into a category with every other straight person who walks the planet? I think you'd probably resist such a label, since you are a unique person, not some clone cut out of straightness.

I think what people really mean by "lifestyle" is—here we go—*sex*. After all, gay and lesbian people live the same lives as straight people. They work, they play, they eat and sleep. Both gay and straight people have gay and straight friends. So when people talk about "the gay lifestyle," what they may really mean is gay sex. But as we'll see, the discussion about homosexuality is much more complex than just a conversation about sex. So let's drop the "lifestyle" lingo.

We also need to be careful about the term *homosexuality*. It's fine to use it; I'll use it throughout our conversation. But we need to be very clear about what we mean. Are we talking about people having sex with someone of the same gender? Or someone just attracted to the same sex? What if they're not acting on their attraction? What if they're not acting on it *now*, but maybe they will in the future? What if someone's actually straight, but they've had same-sex experiences in the past? What if someone is only slightly gay?

"Homosexuality" is a very broad concept that includes many different types of people. So if someone asks you, "What's your view on homosexuality?" ask them what they *mean* by homosexuality before you answer.

I'd recommend never using the word *homosexual* when referring to people. That is, don't use it as a noun, like, "Hey, look at that homosexual." You can say *homosexual* when referring to concepts or things rather than people ("homosexual relationship," "homosexual desires"). But almost every gay person I know does not like to be called "a homosexual." They prefer to be called gay or lesbian. There's no alternative for *bisexual* (someone attracted to both men and women), so that word is okay. Or you could use the well-known acronym LGBT. That is, **L**esbian **G**ay **B**isexual **T**ransgender. Most people tack on a Q for "Queer" (or "Questioning") at the end—LGBTQ. *Queer* is sort of a catchall identifier for everyone else who feels marginalized based on their sexuality. And sometimes there are several other letters added to the mix, like LGBTQTIAP (**L**esbian, **G**ay, **B**isexual, **T**ransgender, **Q**ueer, **T**ranssexual, **I**ntersex, **A**sexual, **P**ansexual) and a long list of others. I tend to just use LGBT or sometimes LGBTQ.

"Transgender," if you're wondering, refers to someone who doesn't identify with his or her biological sex. That person may be a woman on the outside, but they feel like the opposite gender and have the thoughts and emotions of a man, or vice versa. You may wonder, "Isn't that person just a lesbian?" No, they aren't. A lesbian is a woman who feels like a woman, and who's attracted to other women. But a transgender woman identifies as a man (regardless of what their body looks like) and is attracted to women. Or men, in some cases. I know. It gets confusing. We'll talk about all this stuff in chapter 4. When in doubt, just stick to LGBT.

The term *gay* is also used very differently depending on the person using it. When many Christians hear the term *gay*, they immediately think of sexual immorality. But I know many gay people who aren't having sex. The term *gay* is often used as a synonym for "same-sex attraction" (or SSA) and doesn't necessarily mean that the "gay" person is acting on that attraction. We'll talk more about the term *gay* in chapters 6 and 7. For now, I'll use the term *gay* in our conversation as a description of someone who is attracted to the same sex.

There's another set of words that should rarely be used. Words such as "we" versus "they," and "us" versus "them." No one likes to feel like some "other"—a subspecies to the human race. Unfortunately, many gay and lesbians feel like this whenever they hear Christians talk about *"those* gay people" or other such "they/them"-type words. Think about it: Pretend you are fifteen years old and struggling with same-sex attraction. (Some of you don't need to pretend.) You're sitting in the front row at church and the preacher keeps talking about *"those* gay people" and how *"we* need to stand strong against *them"* and *"we* can't let *their* agenda influence *our* children." Whose side would you be on? Even if you desired to be one of "us" (the good, righteous, straight people, who happen to be attracted to the opposite sex), you've just been pushed out to the community of "them." Those nasty, abominable, gay people.

This is not an "us/them" discussion, but very much a "we" discussion. How can *we* best love people who are same-sex attracted among *us*? Who *are* us? Sometimes it's inevitable to use the words "us" or "them." Sometimes the English language demands it. I've even used these terms a few times already, in case you didn't notice! My point is to be very careful about using these terms and to make sure you don't cause people to feel like some less-than-human "other."

A BETTER WAY

Let me be up front and honest about something: I'm not too thrilled with the way many Christians have gone about the "issue" (aah, that term!) of homosexuality. I can always tell whether somebody actually knows a gay person or not. When someone doesn't know a person who's gay, they tend to be harsh, black and white, and factual in their statements.

They quote Bible verses and speak with way too much confidence. And many clearly don't understand, nor do they try to understand, what it may feel like to be sexually attracted to someone of the same sex. Homosexuality is either wrong or right, and since the Bible is clear that it's wrong, they have no patience for those who think otherwise.

That seems to be many Christians these days. But then there's the other side. Those who mockingly discount the Bible as archaic and backwoods—an old-school book for a homeschooled family. How could anyone actually use the Bible to justify their beliefs? Doesn't the Bible also endorse slavery and a flat earth? Can anyone with half a brain still think that the Bible is scientifically credible? Come on, folks! Get with the twenty-first century.

Maybe you've heard some of this before too. Or maybe you've felt the same feelings. Let me be frank: I think both approaches are wrong. The dehumanizing, backwoods, "homosexuality is an abomination, *period*" approach is wrong. And the atheistic, arrogant, "I have no authority but science, myself, and Oprah" approach is wrong too.

I want to take a more balanced approach. It's the more difficult path, but it's one that seeks truth *and* love, conviction *and* compassion. I want to listen to the Bible and take seriously the words of my Creator. And I also want to sit down with a cup of coffee and ask Jordan what it feels like to be treated like an animal at the zoo. We can love people *and* still ask hard questions. Love and truth aren't at odds.

So let's get to some of those questions I mentioned earlier. The first question we're going to ask is this: Are all types of homosexual relations wrong? More specifically, does the Bible prohibit a loving, faithful, committed gay couple from getting married? So we're not asking about people having sex before marriage, or multiple partners. (I take it for granted that the Bible asserts sex outside of marriage is wrong and that bouncing around from lover to lover is sin.) But what about two men ot two women who love each other, who love Jesus and who are committed to lifelong faithfulness? Is anything wrong with that?

To find out, let's crack open the Bible and see what it says. I think you might be surprised.

CHAPTER TWO

WHAT DOES THE BIBLE SAY ABOUT MARRIAGE?

INTRODUCTION

Over the next couple chapters, we're going to talk about what the Bible says about marriage and homosexuality. But first, I want to look at two common reasons people give for saying that same-sex relations are totally fine.

First, many people say, "If two people love each other, and if they are not hurting anyone, then why is it wrong for them to get married?" I'm sure you've probably heard this too. Perhaps you have even thought the same thing. On the surface, the question seems like a no-brainer (slam dunk) for those who affirm same-sex relations. After all, if two guys or two girls are committed to each other, express mutual love for one another, and are not having sex outside of marriage, then why shouldn't they get married? They are not hurting anyone by exchanging vows. And what they do in the bedroom is no one's business.

And then there's the "born this way" argument. Some think that since people are born gay, God must have made them this way. And if God made them this way, then being gay must be okay. After all, why would God create someone to be gay and then turn around and say, "You shouldn't be gay!"

Even though these arguments are common, they are actually bad arguments. Let's look at the first one.

IF TWO PEOPLE LOVE EACH OTHER

"If two people love each other and they're not hurting anyone else, then why shouldn't they get married?" This has been one of the primary arguments in favor of same-sex relations. To forbid same-sex couples from getting married is to stand in the way of love.

I don't think this is a bad question. I only think that it's not the only question that needs to be answered. In other words, even if two people love each other and aren't hurting anyone else, this doesn't in itself mean that they should get married. There are other questions that we need to ask.

For instance, we need to ask questions about God's purpose and design for gender difference, marriage, and sex. Or more specifically: Why has God created humans as two different biological sexes—male and female—and what purpose do these have for marriage and sex? If we believe there's a Creator, and we believe that he designed us as humans—gendered humans who are created male or female—then it only makes sense to ask the question: *Why has God created us male and female, and what does this have to do with sex and marriage?*

I'm not going to answer this question just yet. I only bring it up to show that there are other questions about marriage, sex, and gender that we need to think through before we answer the question about same-sex couples. Whether two people love each other is only one of *several* questions that need to be answered.

We also need to be consistent in how we answer the question above about two people loving each other. After all, most Christians would agree that two people who love each other shouldn't have sex until they've gotten married. But think about it: What if they really love each other and aren't hurting anyone else? *Why* should they not have sex? You may say, "Well, they need to get married first," and I would agree. But *why*? Why do you believe they should get married first? What's your source of authority for your view?

My guess is that you'll probably say something like: Because that's the way God designed sex; it's supposed to take place in the context of marriage, even if two unmarried people love each other.

In other words, two unmarried people shouldn't have sex, because their Creator has designed sex to take place within the covenant of marriage.

Or consider divorce. What if a married couple who doesn't have any kids "fall out of love" with each other and "fall in love" with other people? Is it okay for them to get divorced since they love other people and aren't hurting anyone by getting divorced? Some of you may say, "Sure, why not!" But the Bible is pretty clear that divorce is only allowed under certain circumstances and "falling out of love" with each other isn't one of them.

Again, a married couple who falls out of love should not get divorced, because their Creator has not designed marriage to be broken so easily.

You see, when it comes to questions surrounding sex, marriage, divorce, and, of course, homosexuality, the question "if two people love each other and aren't hurting anyone" isn't the only one we should ask. We also must ask: *What does our Creator say about sex, marriage, and same-sex relations?* This is why we're going to spend the next couple chapters looking at what the Bible says about these topics. After all, the Bible does not just contain religious thoughts about God. Rather, the Bible is God's timeless revelation of himself to mankind. And in it, God reveals to us how he wants us to behave. Sometimes he explains *why* we should do this and not do that, and sometimes he doesn't. (Sometimes as a parent, I do the same thing.) Either way, Christians should submit to what the Bible says about right and wrong—especially when it comes to love, marriage, and sex. Part of being a Christian means believing that God knows what's best for us. We are often our own worst moral guides. If humans were allowed to do whatever they thought was right, then . . . well . . . that would be pretty scary.

DOES GOD MAKE SOME PEOPLE GAY?

People have debated this question for years. It's often called the "nature" versus "nurture" debate. The *nature* side says that people are born with same-sex attraction, while the *nurture* side says that such attraction is developed later on in life. Those who believe that people are born with same-sex attraction (nature) say that if someone is born with it, then it must be okay. Others argue that same-sex attraction is formed by a person's upbringing (nurture). Perhaps they were sexually abused as a kid, or maybe their dad wasn't around growing up and so they grew attached to their mom. Therefore, in their minds, people aren't born gay. Rather, same-sex attraction is developed over time.

I actually think that both views aren't quite correct. Most experts say that both nature and nurture play a role in forming same-sex desires. Some of you may have heard of studies that have "proven" that same-sex attraction comes from *nature*. Or maybe you've heard of other studies that have shown that it comes from *nurture*. I won't get into all the details, but I have read a lot of these studies and the one thing I can say is this: *All of the studies that argue strongly for either nature or nurture have been debunked.* Whenever you hear stuff through the grapevine, or receive forwarded emails from your grandma or whomever, you shouldn't immediately believe it. There's a lot of weird stuff out there, especially on the Internet. So if you're really interested in the nature versus nurture question, I'd recommend doing a lot of reading on both sides of the debate.

But to save you some time, here's the conclusion that was issued by the American Psychological Association (APA), which is agreed upon by leading Christian psychologists. After sifting through all the evidence, the APA says that both *nature* and *nurture* have a part in creating SSA:

There is no consensus among scientists about the exact reasons that an individual develops a heterosexual,

33

bisexual, gay or lesbian orientation. Although much research has examined the possible genetic, hormonal, developmental, social and cultural influences on sexual orientation, no findings have emerged that permit scientists to conclude that sexual orientation is determined by any particular factor or factors. Many think that nature and nurture both play complex roles; most people experience little or no sense of choice about their sexual orientation.[1]

Notice the last sentence: "Many think nature and nurture both play complex roles." In other words, it's unlikely that all gay people were simply "born gay." It's much more complicated than that. It's also unlikely that all gay people became attracted to the same sex through certain experiences growing up (like sexual abuse). It's usually a blend of both *nature* and *nurture*.

But even if all the research showed that same-sex desires are biological (which it doesn't), this still doesn't mean that it's okay to act on those desires. Think about it. The Bible says that people are born with a sinful nature. And this sin nature affects our whole being. Yes, even our desires (Jeremiah 13:13; 17:1, 9; Ephesians 2:3). We all have different dispositions, cravings, and longings that have been messed up through sin.

As a heterosexual male, I have a desire to lust. Others have inborn desires to get angry or eat too much or eat too little. Children born to moms who smoked too much crack while they were pregnant will probably be born with a desire for crack. But this doesn't make it right to act on those desires.

---

1   www.apa.org/topics/lgbt/orientation.aspx, under dropdown category, "What causes a person to have a particular sexual orientation?"

I love how Justin Lee puts it:

We all have inborn tendencies to sin in any number of ways. If gay people's same-sex attractions were inborn, that wouldn't necessarily mean it's okay to act on them, and if we all agreed that gay sex is sinful, that wouldn't necessarily mean that same-sex attractions aren't inborn. "Is it a sin?" and "Does it have biological roots?" are two completely separate questions.[2]

I think Justin is spot on here. And Justin is the leader of the Gay Christian Network. This means that the whole "God made me this way" argument could help his cause. But Justin believes what he said. He agrees with the Bible. He believes that our desires are tainted by sin and are terrible instructors of morality. The fact that people have same-sex desires does not change the ethical question: Is it God's will for people to act on those desires?

GOD'S WILL

So what does God say about acting on same-sex desires?

Now let me be honest with you. I grew up believing that the Bible says that homosexual behavior is sin. The fact is, though, I simply adopted this view from my pastors and my parents. My belief about homosexuality didn't actually come directly from the Bible. That is, until a few years ago

---

2   Justin Lee, *Torn: Rescuing the Gospel from the Gays-vs.-Christians Debate* (New York: Jericho, 2012), 62.

when I started studying what the Bible actually says about homosexuality. I tried to study the Bible with an open mind. I didn't want to just use the Bible to prove my presuppositions. I wanted to know what the Bible actually says—even if it ended up correcting the view I grew up with.

I want us to read the Bible with this perspective now. We need to look at what the Bible actually says about homosexuality. We shouldn't make the Bible say what we want it to say, and we shouldn't assume that we know what it's going to say. Can you do that? Will you go where the Bible leads you? If the Bible is our authority—and if you're a Christian, it should be—then we should be willing to believe and embrace what the Bible says about homosexuality.

I'm not going to tell you what to believe. I'm not going to spoon-feed you the "right answer." What I'm going to do is simply point out some basic truths in the Bible that will help guide our thinking about homosexuality. As we go through the Bible, our discussion might feel pretty in-depth. Or for some of you, it might feel pretty light! It all depends on how familiar you are with the Bible and the passages that address homosexuality. Anyway, if you want more depth or if you still have more questions about the text, I've included an even deeper discussion in the appendix.

WHAT THE BIBLE SAYS ABOUT MARRIAGE

Let's first start by looking at what the Bible says about marriage. Genesis 2 gives a basic design for marriage, especially

2:8–25. Here, God creates Adam, and when he sees that Adam is alone, God creates a woman named Eve to be his wife. And if you look at Genesis 2:24, you'll see that Adam and Eve's marriage was a general blueprint for all marriages that follow. Look at what it says:

> That's why a man leaves his father and mother and is joined to his wife. The two of them become one. (Genesis 2:24)

Genesis 2 isn't just about Adam and Eve, nor is it just about their marriage. It's about God's design for all marriages. But that doesn't mean that all marriages should look just like Adam and Eve's. After all, running around naked in a garden might seem fun during the summertime. But do we all have to imitate Adam and Eve's choice of clothing—or lack thereof? Some aspects of Adam and Eve's marriage are better left in the garden.

But some might still be for today. So the main question for our topic is: Does Genesis 2:24 automatically rule out same-sex marriages? Does this verse by itself mean that all future marriages must be between a man and a woman?

Well, not quite. At least, not by itself. Just because Genesis 2 affirms a heterosexual marriage doesn't mean that all marriages must be heterosexual. For instance, I can say that I love the Dodgers and this doesn't in itself rule out the possibility that I also love the Giants. Likewise, God can create an opposite-sex marriage in Genesis 2 and this doesn't necessarily rule out the possibility that there's a place for homosexual marriages.

If I were a judge in a court of law and I was examining the

biblical evidence for homosexual marriages, I don't know if I would smack my gavel on the bench just yet—I would need to see more evidence. And I would have other questions, like "How do we know Genesis 2 must exclude same-sex unions? Same-sex unions aren't mentioned here at all, so how do we know they're prohibited? Maybe God created Eve for Adam so that they could procreate and populate the earth. Perhaps after the earth was populated, gay marriages would then be allowed."

You can see how Genesis 2 doesn't in itself solve the question. But it does at least point in the direction of heterosexual marriages as the norm.

Jesus on Marriage

However, Jesus says something later on that does seem to say that marriage should be between a man and a woman. Look at what he says:

> "He who created them from the beginning made them male and female, and said, 'Therefore a man shall leave his father and his mother and hold fast to his wife, and the two shall become one flesh.'" (Matthew 19:4–5 ESV)

Notice that Jesus doesn't just say that "two *people* should become one flesh," but explicitly says *male* and *female*. When Jesus appeals to God's design for marriage, he says that marriage is between a *male* and a *female*. In fact, Jesus even quotes from both Genesis 1 and Genesis 2 in this passage. This shows that Jesus rooted his view of marriage in Genesis 1 and 2.

Paul on Marriage

The apostle Paul says something similar in Ephesians 5: A husband and wife become "one flesh" when they get married. Only here, Paul compares the husband and wife's union to the relationship between Christ and the church. The Bible often compares human marriages to God's relationship with his people. In the Old Testament, it was between God and Israel. In the New Testament, it's between Christ and the church. So Paul says that husband and wife reflect Christ and the church in their marriage.

Why is this significant? Well, the comparison wouldn't make good sense if the human marriage were between a husband and a husband, or a wife and a wife. Think about it. The difference between Christ and the church is reflected in *the difference between a husband and wife.*

Again, like Jesus's statement on marriage, *male* and *female* appears to be significant.

Now, we want to be careful. Neither Jesus nor Paul were responding to homosexuality when they talked about marriage. It's not as if a gay couple walked up to Jesus and said, "Hey, Jesus, do you think it's cool if we get married?" Jesus was actually talking about divorce when he said that marriage is between male and female. And Paul doesn't bring up homosexuality when he talks about marriage in Ephesians 5.

But I still think that the three passages we've looked at—Genesis 2, Matthew 19, and Ephesians 5—assume that marriage is between a man and a woman. Every time marriage is talked about positively, it's always between a man and a woman. This isn't a slam-dunk, end-of-story, case-closed reason to believe that same-sex marriages are outside of God's will. But it should cause people to stop and think.

If God affirms same-sex couples, you would expect that the Bible would say something positive about same-sex relationships. We'll tackle this question next in our conversation. But first, let's sum up what we've seen so far.

1. The argument that "if two people love each other and aren't hurting anyone, then they should get married" isn't a very good argument.

2. The assumption that "since God makes people gay, it must be okay" is both scientifically naïve and biblically wrong.

3. The marriage between Adam and Eve in Genesis 2 reveals aspects of God's design for all marriages.

4. Jesus and Paul quote Genesis 2 and assume that marriage should be between a man and a woman.

What do you think? Do these four points automatically rule out same-sex marriages? Personally, I need more evidence. After all, homosexuality is an important issue, since *people* are important. I don't want to say that God doesn't affirm same-sex couples unless I'm very confident that God has said so in his Word. And I encourage you to have this same posture. Think deeply about everything I'm saying. Don't check your mind at the door. Study it for yourself. Do the hard work and evaluate the things I'm saying. Don't be convinced by a few arguments. Look at all the evidence and resist coming to a quick conclusion. After all, none of the passages we've looked at explicitly mention same-sex marriages or same-sex couples. If I were you, I would want to know if there are any passages that explicitly mention same-sex relations.

Indeed there are. But don't worry; it won't take too long to look at them all. After all, there are only six passages that mention homosexuality—three in the Old Testament and three in the New Testament. Let's check these out.

CHAPTER THREE

WHAT DOES THE BiBLE SAY ABOUT HOMOSEXUALITY?

Let's continue our conversation by talking about the six passages in the Bible that explicitly mention homosexual relations. Even though there are only a few passages, we need to look at them carefully to make sure we understand them correctly.

SODOM AND GOMORRAH

The first passage is famous. It's the story about Sodom and Gomorrah, and it goes like this.

Two men visit the city of Sodom, and Lot (Abraham's nephew) takes them into his home. All of a sudden, the men of the city come banging on Lot's door and shouting: "Where are the men who came to you tonight? Bring them out to us. We want to have sex with them" (Genesis 19:5).

Lot goes outside to urge the men not to harm his guests. He even offers up his two virgin daughters so the men won't harm his guests. (I'm not sure what to do with that.) But this only makes the mob mad. "'Get out of our way!' the men of Sodom replied" (19:9). The men get ready to bum-rush the door when suddenly Lot's two guests strike the men with blindness.

Come to find out, Lot's guests weren't ordinary men. They were actually angels who appeared as men. Either way, the men who surrounded Lot's door that night tried to have sex with these two angels, who they thought were men.

So what does this story teach us about homosexuality?

Before we answer that question, notice two things. First, no one had sex with anyone. The men wanting to have sex were shot down, or at least struck down, by the men inside. While they certainly wanted to have sex, they never even got to first base.

Second, the men of Sodom attempted to gang rape Lot's guests. There was no courting, no flowers, no dates, no flirting. Just attempted sexual violence by a bunch of men.

So what does this story say about homosexuality? Well, not much. If the story of Sodom teaches us anything, it's that attempted gang rape is wrong. It doesn't tell us much of anything about two men falling in love and wanting to get married. In fact, the men of Sodom probably weren't even gay. At least, they weren't gay in the modern sense of the term. You see, in Old Testament times, men would sometimes rape other men in order to show them who was boss. It was an act of domination, not attraction. The same sort of thing goes on in prisons today. One dude will make another dude "his woman," but it has nothing to do with attraction or love.

But again, the question we're asking is: Can two people of the same sex fall in love, get married, and have sex? And in regard to that question, the story about Sodom tells us nothing.

In fact, whenever the Bible talks about the "sin of Sodom," it *never* mentions homosexuality. The Bible usually describes Sodom as a city that was greedy and prideful. Check out Ezekiel:

> "Here is the sin your sister Sodom committed. She and her daughters were proud. They ate too much. They were not concerned about others. They did not help those who were poor and in need. They were very proud." (Ezekiel 16:49–50)

Wow! Did you get that? Ezekiel says that the real sin of Sodom was that they were overfed, arrogant, and unconcerned for the poor. It's pretty sad when overfed, greedy Christians who perfectly fit Ezekiel's description run around hating on gay people. In fact, the Bible gives a different picture of who the real "Sodomites" are. Many of them are overstuffed straight people.

So in the end, the story of Sodom tells us that attempted gang rape is wrong, but it doesn't tell us much about loving, consensual same-sex relations.

LEVITICUS

The next two verses that mention same-sex relations come from Leviticus:

> "Do not have sex with a man as you would have sex with a woman. I hate that." (Leviticus 18:22)

"Suppose a man has sex with another man as he would have sex with a woman. I hate what they have done. They must be put to death. Anything that happens to them will be their own fault." (Leviticus 20:13)

Leviticus is a strange book. It's filled with rules about tattoos, menstruation, and not eating mole rats. Seriously, it's all there. Maybe that's why gay people get frustrated when Christians use Leviticus to condemn homosexuality. Are we ready to obey *everything* in this book? Yikes! That means we'd have to give up eating mole rats . . .

I've got to admit, when I first studied these passages, my first reaction was to toss them aside with the rest of Leviticus and move on to the "more important" verses in the New Testament. But then I decided to sit down and read the passages carefully. And when I did, I realized that these two verses shouldn't be dismissed so easily.

Notice that there's no mention of rape, attempted violence, or anything else that we saw in the Sodom story. No one is trying to force another person into having sex. In Leviticus 20:13, if two men sleep with each other, they are *both* condemned. The fact that both of them are punished shows that the act was consensual. If the verses were talking about some sort of ancient "prison rape," only the rapist would have been condemned.

Now, what about the fact that these verses are in Leviticus? After all, Leviticus also condemns eating catfish, wearing poly-cotton blends, and shaving the edges of your beard. So why obey two verses about same-sex relations?

This is actually a good point. Christians need to figure out which Old Testament laws we're supposed to obey. Some laws are meant to apply today, and some aren't because they may have been written for a very specific reason and context. But here's the thing. When it comes to who (or what) we're allowed to have sex with, *all* the laws in the Old Testament are still valid. Just scan through the rest of Leviticus 18, the so-called "sex chapter." You'll see that God gives us tons of rules about sex partners. It tells us not to have sex with our brother, sister, mother, father, aunt, uncle, and so on. It also tells us not to have sex with animals. Not to have sex with another man's wife. And not to sacrifice our kids to foreign gods. No one disputes whether these laws are for today.

Even if we widen our scope and look at all of the laws in Leviticus 18–20, we see that almost every law is still valid. Stealing, lying, cheating, slandering, witchcraft, pimping your daughter out for sex, and many other laws in Leviticus 18–20 are still to be obeyed. There are only a few laws in these chapters that aren't for today, but those are very clear. Again, when it comes to marriage and sex, the Bible only endorses opposite sex partners from different families.

Now, if you're still wondering whether Leviticus 18:22 and 20:13 are still for today, the most fail-proof test is to see if an Old Testament law is repeated in the New Testament. Cheating, lying, stealing—it's all repeated in the New. Adultery, murder, drunkenness. Yup, it's all there. But what about eating pork? Leviticus forbids it, but the New Testament says that Christians don't need to obey this law. The same goes for animal sacrifices. We don't need to sacrifice lambs at church today because the Old Testament sacrificial laws were fulfilled in Christ.

So what does the New Testament say about same-sex relations? Let's find out.

JESUS ON HOMOSEXUALITY

You may be surprised to know that Jesus never mentions homosexuality. Not once. He talked about many sins and even talked about sexual sins, like adultery, lust, and divorce. But he never mentions same-sex relations.

Now you can take this in one of three ways. You could say that Jesus must have been perfectly fine with homosexuality since he never talked about it. But this is a bad assumption. After all, Jesus never mentioned rape, incest, or bestiality (having sex with animals), but this doesn't mean that he was totally cool with those things.

Jesus's silence also doesn't mean he was undecided or indifferent on the issue. Some people think that if Jesus *were* asked about same-sex relations, he would have shrugged his messianic shoulders and said, "I don't care about that stuff! As long as you're not hurting anyone, then go for it."

I'm not sure this is how Jesus would have responded.

The third possible reason Jesus never mentions same-sex relations is because the question never came up. After all, most of the people he talked to were Jews, and religious Jews in Jesus's day had only one opinion on the matter: Same-sex relations were sin. Period.

I think this third reason is probably the best one. Jesus never addressed same-sex relations because this wasn't an issue among Jewish people.

Plus, as we have seen, the Old Testament is pretty clear about same-sex relations. Since they are prohibited in the Old Testament, and since all Jewish people in Jesus's day knew this, the question never came up.

We could compare this to polygamy today. At least in America, polygamy is so rare that most Christian pastors don't feel the need to preach on it. In fact, I've been preaching for more than twenty years and I've never preached a sermon on polygamy. Does this mean that I'm for it? Or indifferent toward it? "Hey, man, if it works for you, then go for it!" Probably not.

Silence doesn't mean affirmation. And silence doesn't mean indifference. There are good, historical reasons why Jesus never mentioned homosexuality. He simply didn't need to.

ROMANS 1

But Paul did. Unlike Jesus, who ministered mainly to Jews, Paul's main audience was Gentiles. And homosexual relations were widespread in Paul's Gentile world. Paul mentions some sort of same-sex sexual relations in three different passages. The first one comes in Romans 1, and it goes like this:

So God let them continue to have their shameful desires.
Their women committed sexual acts that were not natural.
In the same way, the men turned away from their natural

love for women. They burned with sexual desire for each other. Men did shameful things with other men. They suffered in their bodies for all the wrong things they did. (Romans 1:26–27)

This is the clearest statement about homosexuality in the Bible. Let's look at a few things that Paul says in this passage.

First, Paul says that both female and male homosexual *sex* is "not natural." Notice that he doesn't say that gay *people* are "not natural" or abominations or creepy or weird or disgusting. All people are created in God's image and are beautiful in his sight. We should never make people feel like they are worthless or shameful before God. All people are precious in God's sight. But sometimes we do things that are sinful, shameful, or in this case "not natural."

Second, if you look at the end of the chapter, Paul goes on to mention a whole pile of sins that are committed by all people. Yes, even you.

They want more than they need. They commit murder. They want what belongs to other people. They fight and cheat. They hate others. They say mean things about other people. They tell lies about them. They hate God. They are rude and proud. They brag. They think of new ways to do evil. They don't obey their parents. They do not understand. They can't be trusted. They are not loving and kind. (Romans 1:29–31)

Wow. Did you make the list? Yeah, I did too. The fact is, we are all sinners in need of grace. Paul later says, "Everyone is under the power of sin" (Romans 3:9), and "Everyone has sinned. No one measures up to God's glory" (Romans 3:23). That's the whole point of the first three chapters of Romans. Everyone has messed up, and that's why we all—gay and straight—need Jesus. We need to keep this in mind when we talk about homosexuality. We are all like beggars showing other beggars where to find bread.

So Romans 1 lists homosexual sex as one of many sins that people commit. We shouldn't consider gay people as "others" but as one of "us."

Third, Romans 1 doesn't just talk about abusive or nonconsensual same-sex acts. He says that "they burned with sexual desire *for each other*" and "they suffered in their bodies for all the wrong things *they* did" (Romans 1:26–27). As far as we can tell, Paul is talking about mutual sex. He's not singling out rape, or pedophilia (sex with children), or prostitution. He's talking about partners in a mutual relationship. He's talking about two people of the same gender having sex. And he says that it's "not natural."

Fourth, the phrase "not natural" doesn't mean that something is weird or creepy. It means that same-sex intercourse goes against the design of Creator God. In fact, if you look at the previous verses (Romans 1:18–23), you'll see that Paul's whole point is focused on people going against God's design of creation. God designed males to have marital sex with females. Even if some males or females desire to have sex with people of the same gender, this doesn't mean that it's okay. It goes against nature—the way God designed us.

Have you hit informational overload yet?

Why don't we pause for a second, catch our breath, and remind ourselves one more time that we're not just talking about some issue. We're not collecting Bible verses so that we can win an argument with our friends about homosexuality. We're considering the real pain and daily desires of people created in God's image. If you're straight, then you have your own issues that you deal with daily. So don't be a judgmental hypocrite and look down your nose at people who struggle with same-sex attraction. And if you're the one struggling with same-sex attraction, you're not in sin unless you act on it. Even if you do act on it, there's forgiveness through Jesus for those who repent of their sin. God doesn't look at you like some despicable person, even if some people have made you feel this way. God not only delights in you, he delights in forgiving your sin. And there's no greater joy in the heart of God than welcoming all types of people into his kingdom.

We need to read these verses with tears in our eyes. Tears of sorrow over the bitter struggle that we all have over our sin. And tears of joy over Jesus, who has triumphed over all of our sin. The homosexuality question is first and foremost about beautiful people loved by God.

With that in mind, let's look at the last two passages that mention same-sex behavior.

In 1 Corinthians 6, Paul mentions same-sex behavior in a list of sins.

> Don't you know that people who do wrong will not receive
> God's kingdom? Don't be fooled. Those who commit

sexual sins will not receive the kingdom. Neither will those who worship statues of gods or commit adultery. Neither will men who sleep with other men. Neither will thieves or those who always want more and more. Neither will those who are often drunk or tell lies or cheat. People who live like that will not receive God's kingdom. (1 Corinthians 6:9–10)

Like in Romans 1, Paul doesn't just single out gay people here. He lists same-sex *behavior* in a list of other sins such as adultery, stealing, greed, and drunkenness. Are you beginning to see a pattern? Same-sex intercourse is one of many sins. Those who commit this sin are no worse off than the other seven billion straight people who walk the earth. We all need Jesus.

In 1 Corinthians 6, Paul focuses again on the *act* of homosexual sex. And he's not just talking about one act or two acts. He's not talking about Christians who mess up, feel bad, and turn from their sin. He's talking about people who are completely given over to a sinful act. Drunks who never turn from their sin. Adulterers who keep sleeping around with other people's spouses. And men (he doesn't mention women here) who persistently have sex with other males.

Unless they repent and turn to Jesus, they will not inherit the kingdom of God.

The last passage is 1 Timothy 1:

We also know that the law isn't made for godly people. [. . .] It is for those who commit sexual sins. It is for those who commit homosexual acts. It is for people who buy and sell slaves. It is for liars. It is for people who tell lies in court. It is for those who are a witness to things that aren't true. And it is for anything else that is the opposite of true teaching. (1 Timothy 1:9–10)

As you can see, this passage is a lot like the previous one. Paul mentions several sins that we need to repent from, including "homosexual acts," which refers to sexual acts. He's not talking about people who struggle with same-sex attraction, or who repent after they mess up. He's talking about willful, persistent sin. And once again, these same-sex acts are stuffed in a context where many other sins are mentioned.

SUMMARY

Let's sum up what we've seen so far in the Bible. In the previous chapter, we saw that:

1. The argument that "if two people love each other and aren't hurting anyone, then they should get married" isn't a very good argument.

2. The argument that "since God makes people gay, it must be okay" is a bad one.

3. The marriage between Adam and Eve in Genesis 2 reveals God's design for marriage.

4. Jesus and Paul quote Genesis 2 and assume that marriage should be between a man and a woman.

In this chapter, we looked at the six passages that explicitly mention homosexual sex, and we found that:

1. The story of Sodom (Genesis 19) talks about attempted gang rape and not consensual same-sex relations. It's therefore irrelevant for our topic.

2. Leviticus 18 forbids all forms of same-sex male relations. It's not limited to rape or prostitution, and it still seems to be relevant for today.

3. Romans 1 says both male and female homosexual acts are sin.

4. 1 Corinthians 6 and 1 Timothy 1 list same-sex acts in a list of other sins.

In light of these observations, it does seem pretty clear that the Bible forbids homosexual sex. Again, I've tried to read these passages fairly. I'm trying hard not to read a particular view into the text. I have a lot of gay and lesbian friends, and there's a big part of me that would love to see them fall in love with someone of the same gender. And many people would say that it's very *unloving* to say they can't.

But think about this. Is it really unloving?

To me, it's only unloving if God says it's fine. But after looking at several key passages, we've seen that God doesn't say it's fine. And since God has not designed us to have sexual relations with people of the same sex—even if we desire to—then it's actually *unloving* to encourage them to. Our human desires are very poor moral guides for determining right and wrong. We must look to our Creator, who knows us better than we know ourselves, and submit to what *he* says about how we are to live.

CHAPTER FOUR

GENDER, TRANSGENDER, AND INTERSEX

My friend Lesli was born a female. She had all the biological parts that made her a girl. But from the time she was four years old, she felt like a boy. She had emotions like a boy, played like a boy, and even thought that her girl body would one day transform into a boy body. Lesli didn't make a conscious choice to feel like a boy. The feeling just sort of came upon her at a young age and stuck with her throughout life.

You may think that Lesli is gay. But actually, she is transgender. And the two are not always the same.

If you've been paying attention to the culture around you, you've noticed that discussions surrounding transgender (sometimes called transsexual) people are just as common as homosexuality. Television shows, such as Netflix's *Orange Is the New Black* or Amazon's rather raunchy *Transparent*, showcase transgender people. The famous broadcast journalist Barbara Walters ran a controversial story a few years ago about a transgender child named Jazz, who though born as a boy shows every sign of being a girl. Google the story and you'll see what I mean. You would *never* be able to tell that Jazz is biologically a boy. And, of course, there's the recent story about former Olympian—and former hubby to Kris Kardashian—Bruce (now Caitlyn) Jenner, whose transition from male to female has been highly publicized throughout 2015.

So what does "transgender" mean? And how is it different from homosexuality?

The technical phrase for being transgender is gender identity disorder, or more popularly gender dysphoria. The term *dysphoria* simply means to be dissatisfied or uneasy about something. So gender dysphoria means that someone is dissatisfied about their gender. Like Lesli, they were born into a female body but everything about them feels male (or simply *not* female). Or vice versa. This is what transgender means. A transgender person *identifies with a gender that is different from the one into which they were born.*

So how does a transgender person differ from a gay person? Basically, a *gay* man identifies as a man but is sexually attracted to other men. But a *transgender* man may have been born into a male body and identifies as a female. He—or she—may be sexually attracted to other men, or may be attracted to other women.

Do you see the difference? It gets confusing, I know. Just to be clear, a gay person says they're gay because of whom they're *attracted to*, while a transgender person identifies as transgender based on the gender they *identify with*.

Now let's introduce a few other terms that are sometimes confused with the term *transgender*.

Transsexual is often used as a synonym for *transgender.* Usually, though, *transsexual* refers to a transgender person who has had a sex change, or sexual reassignment surgery (SRS). This can be done through medicine (hormone treatment) and surgery, where the genitalia of your body is replaced with the genitalia of the gender you identify with. But this is important: *Not every transgender person has had a sex change.* Some do and some don't. So if you know someone who says they're transgender, they still may have the genitalia they were born with.

The term *transvestite* is often confused with *transgender,* but they are not the same. A transvestite is someone who dresses in the clothes of the opposite sex—a man wearing makeup and a skirt or a woman wearing a man's suit. Stuff like that. Now, a transgender person may also be a transvestite, and a transvestite may be transgender. But this isn't always the case. It's important to distinguish these two terms.

And then there's the term *intersex.* An intersex person is someone who was born with ambiguous genitalia, or perhaps a blend of both male and female parts. The older term for this was *hermaphrodite,* but *intersex* is the proper term to use today.

Are you getting all of this? I know, it's a lot to take in, especially if this is your first time coming across these terms. My guess, though, is that you've probably already heard of them. Since we're talking about various terms, we might as well make sure we also understand the difference between *sex* and *gender.* And by sex I mean the biological sex of a person; not "having sex."

Sex refers to the biological sex of a person, while *gender* refers to one's sense and expression of being male or female. Sometimes people use the term *gender* to refer to the biological sex of a person. In fact, in case you've noticed, I've done this a few times in our conversation. But technically, *gender* refers to the sense of being male or female, while *sex* is the biological anatomy of their body.

Okay, are we good? There's a lot of stuff we could talk about here, but let's just focus on two of the terms we mentioned above: transgender and intersex. How should Christians think about such people?

TRANSGENDER

I've tried to learn as much as I can about gender dysphoria, but it's been very tough! I don't claim to have it all figured out. But again, I'm not trying to lecture at you. We're just having a conversation. So in our conversation about transgender and intersex people, I'm going to raise some questions, look at some biblical passages, and try to make sense of it all. My only goal, though, is to get you to think compassionately and biblically about this pressing issue. I mean . . . about *people*.

So what are we to think of people who feel like they've been born into the wrong body?

Our first response must be one of compassion. Let's continue with Lesli's story. Even though she thought she was born into the wrong body, she also accepted Jesus at a young age and loved him with all her heart. It wasn't until her teenage years that she realized she didn't fit the mold of who people wanted her to be. She realized then that she was transgender—biologically female but everything else male.

Lesli continued to love Jesus and was passionately involved at her church. But toward the end of her freshman year in high school, her pastor began preaching on homosexuality, and this is when her world fell apart. Here's what she told me:

> My pastor began a sermon series that included the evils of homosexuality. He condemned all homosexuals to hell. God had no forgiveness for such deviants. Even worse was the mentally ill transgender community. He spoke in detail about men becoming women and women becoming men. These people were an abomination in God's eyes. They were un-savable. We must protect our children from their evil ploys. My friends shouted "Amen" and showed appropriate levels of disgust . . . I was ashamed that I was such an abomination to the God that I adored.

Read that last line again and put yourself in Lesli's shoes. She was *ashamed that she was such an abomination to the God that she adored.* Have you ever felt like that? Maybe you don't identify with Lesli's gender dysphoria. But maybe you feel ashamed about your body. Your personality. Your face. Your family. Your hair, or poverty, or friends, or lack of friends. Maybe you've turned to pornography to satisfy your lust. Or perhaps you're starving your body or cutting your flesh or contemplating skipping town since no one understands you. Or maybe you're thinking about suicide.

The fact is, most of us go through times when we *feel* like Lesli did: Ashamed. Unloved. Lonely. Depressed. You may not be transgender, but you can still identify with her pain. And when we are able to identify with someone's pain, it's much easier to have compassion on them—on people like Lesli.

Lesli was convinced that neither the church nor that church's god accepted her, so she did what thousands of LGBT people have done: she left the church and tried to find love in the LGBT community.

Thanks to the grace of God, many years later another pastor reached out to Lesli and welcomed her into his church. Lesli came back to Christ and now helps teens who are wrestling with their gender identity. But many LGBT individuals haven't come back. They remain bitter at the church—or scared of Christians—because it was in the church where they felt the most pain. They keep hearing about some "gospel" papered over with a thin veneer of grace, but it's a gospel that lacks compassion. A gospel that feels like hypocrisy and judgmentalism.

This has led me to believe we must have compassion on people who identify with the opposite gender into which they were born.

But having compassion doesn't mean that we affirm everyone's behavior and feelings. Our feelings are just as sinful as everything else within us. Even though a girl feels like a boy, or a boy like a girl, doesn't mean that those feelings reflect God's will for that person. This is important to understand. Many people say that the *biological sex* of transgender people is wrong and their *perception of who they are* is right. But the Bible doesn't say that our perceptions of ourselves are always right. Many times they are wrong.

In no way do I want to downplay the real pain that transgender people go through when they feel like the opposite gender. I want to empathize with them. Cry with them. Listen to their pain and hopes and fears and joys. But this doesn't mean that their perceptions accurately reflect God's perception of them.

It's not a perfect analogy, but think about people who struggle with anorexia. I've seen an eighty-pound adult woman look into the mirror and say she's fat. And so she starves herself to lose weight. But no one would say that her perception of herself must be correct. Her eighty-pound biology suggests otherwise. She's a rail. And she needs to eat. She's not fat. Those are the facts—regardless of what *she* thinks she looks like.

In a similar way, people who are born into a body they don't identify with don't necessarily have the most truthful perception of who they are.

WHAT DOES THE BIBLE SAY ABOUT GENDER DYSPHORIA?

So what does the Bible say about gender dysphoria? Well, not much. Throughout the Bible, people who are born biologically male are expected to act like biological males. And the same goes for females. The Bible only talks about males and females. It doesn't talk about biological males who should live as if they are females.

But we have to be careful when we talk about gender roles. Certainly, different cultures have different expectations for masculinity and femininity. There is no one way to be a man or woman. For instance, I visited the Samoan islands in the South Pacific several years ago. And according to the Samoan culture, men wear skirts. (And real men go commando when they wear their skirts, which makes it really interesting when the wind picks up! I've got some stories, but I'd rather keep them to myself.) In that culture, it's not feminine to wear a skirt. It's actually masculine. In America, however, the opposite is true.

Now, there's nothing sinful about men wearing skirts. But the Bible does say that biological males should act like biological males—even though what it means to be a man may differ from culture to culture. This is why the Bible forbids cross-dressing. Deuteronomy says, "A woman must not wear men's clothes. And a man must not wear women's clothes. The LORD your God hates it when anyone does this" (22:5). Cross-dressing isn't primarily about the types of fabric that cover your flesh. It's about identifying with a gender that's different from your biological sex. It's a heart issue.

Likewise, Paul says that women should have long hair while men should have short hair, since this was a cultural norm in his day (1 Corinthians 11:2–16). But this isn't the cultural norm in America. While most women have long hair and most men have short hair, no one would assume that a woman is trying to be a man if she has short hair. So the specific rule about long hair doesn't apply today, as hairstyle does not reflect one's gender in the same way it did back then. But the heart of the command does: men and women shouldn't cross gender boundaries.

According to the Bible, men are to act like men, and women are to act like women. But what it means to act like a woman or man will differ depending on the culture.

There's another truth that is sometimes missed when Christians think about gender dysphoria. Again, a transgender person says that they've been born into the wrong body. Their "true self" is different than their "bodily self." I don't deny that people may feel this way. Again, this is exactly how my friend Lesli has felt and continues to feel. But the Bible doesn't say that humans are divided between the "bodily you" and the "spiritual you." The Bible talks about the body and soul (and sometimes the spirit) as different aspects of one whole person (1 Thessalonians 5:23). You don't just *have* a body—a physical shell that covers the *real* you. Rather, you *are* a body. And you don't just have a soul. You *are* a soul. When God breathed life into Adam, the Bible says that he became (literally) "a living *soul*" (Genesis 2:7 KJV). Your body and your soul both constitute the real you.

I don't want to complicate our conversation, but this is an important point to chew on. There was a false teaching that existed in the early church called "Gnosticism." It taught a sort of body-soul dualism that said that our souls are trapped inside our bodies and that true salvation happens when our souls are freed from our bodies. I've actually heard some modern Christians speak this way, but this is a false teaching. Our bodies are good. They were created by God. And when Christ returns, he's going to give us new *bodies*. We're not going to live eternally in some disembodied state. We will have perfect, sinless, yet real fleshly bodies.

So when someone says that their true self has been born into the wrong body, this is simply wrong. Their true self *is* their body.

Now, let's go back to the relationship between gender dysphoria and homosexuality. Although there are some differences between the two, they overlap in one key area: sex. As we have seen, the Bible shows that biological males are not allowed to have sex with biological males, even if one of those males *feels like a female*. One's sense of who they are doesn't trump who their body says they are. So even though a transgender person may not feel gay, they are still forbidden from getting married to, and having sex with, another person of the same biological sex. From God's perspective, same-sex sex (regardless of a person's perceived gender) is "not natural" (Romans 1:26).

Now, it's possible that a person's biological sex has also been affected by sin. Not everyone is born clearly male or female. And this leads us to think about intersex people.

INTERSEX

Approximately one out of every fifteen hundred people is born intersex. That is, they are born with some sort of atypical sexual anatomy. This could range from—sorry to be graphic—an abnormally small penis and low level of testosterone to being born with XY (male) chromosomes yet female genitalia. Are they a boy? Or are they a girl? Sometimes it's tough to tell.

In these cases, the doctor who delivers the baby often decides whether the intersex baby should be a boy or girl. And so he surgically removes the parts that he feels don't belong. But this can get complicated. What if he cuts off the wrong parts? In some ways, the doctors are playing God when they determine which gender the baby will be. What if they misread the ambiguous genitalia? It gets messy, to say the least!

So what are we to make of all of this?

First, the fact that some people are born with ambiguous genitalia should not be surprising. Some people are born with cleft lips, missing limbs, and all sorts of other biological abnormalities. In fact, I was born deaf in my left ear. This doesn't mean that this is the way God created me. What it means is that sin has affected the very fabric of our being, and sometimes it distorts our biology—even from birth. Siamese twins, missing eyes, or even brains attached to the outside of a person's head. These birth defects are products of a fallen world. It shouldn't surprise us that such birth defects can take place in our sexual anatomy.

Again, we must have compassion and empathy for anyone born with ambiguous genitalia, especially if the doctor happened to cut off the wrong parts.

Second, I don't think that intersex people are some sort of "third gender" or blend of male and female. But this is what some people say. There are males, females, and intersex. All three are legitimate sexes. But I don't see how someone could reconcile this with Scripture. Intersex people were around during Bible times; it's not a new phenomenon. But the Bible only recognizes two biological sexes: male and female. There is certainly a lot of diversity about what it means to be male and female—remember, I wore a skirt in Samoa. But such diversity of gender *expression* doesn't mean that there are several different biological sexes. There's nothing in the Bible that talks about a third biological sex.

SUMMARY

Transgender and intersex people are loved by Jesus just like the rest of us. They experience sin like everyone else. Such people—and maybe you're such a person—need to know that despite their dysphoria, despite their ambiguity, despite the fact that they live daily in much confusion and loneliness and pain, God delights in them as a beautiful part of his creation.

God is deeply grieved over his broken creation and longs to restore things back to the way they were. In the afterlife, God will make all things new and he will banish sin from his creation. No longer will people experience gender dysphoria, and no longer will people live in an ambiguous sexual state. In God's new creation, I won't struggle with lust, addiction, pride, greed, selfishness, or any other cancerous invasion into God's good creation. Everything will be set right. Everything will be made new. And we can all join hands in that hope, that whatever pain and confusion we experience in this life, it will all be transformed into eternal bliss.

CHAPTER FIVE

TRUTH AND LOVE

I want to circle back around and look at Jesus. I know I said earlier that Jesus never mentions homosexuality. And this is true. He never mentions it. But there are things Jesus says and does that should help us think better—more Christlike—about same-sex relations.

TRUTHFULLY LOVING, LOVINGLY TRUTHFUL

Many Christians are trying to figure out how to be both truthful and loving toward gay people. I would consider myself one of these Christians, and I hope you do too. Christ always stood on the truth, and yet he always demonstrated love. He was truthfully loving and lovingly truthful. By that I mean he was never unloving with the truth, and never untruthful when he loved.

Jesus is a perfect example of how Christians should relate to people who are gay.

When you look at Jesus, you'll see that he had a high standard of obedience. He wasn't afraid to condemn sin and call people to repent. One of his most famous (and longest!) sermons is the so-called Sermon on the Mount recorded in Matthew 5–7. In it, Jesus says that lust is just as bad as adultery, vengeance is always wrong, and loving your enemy is always right. He condemns divorce, taking oaths, hypocrisy, and being anxious for the future. Jesus had a very high standard of obedience. He wasn't some pot-smoking hippie who affirmed everyone's behavior. He was a strict religious teacher who preached hard-hitting sermons.

Jesus is all about truth. He cared deeply about holiness. But Jesus also welcomed the worst of sinners with unconditional love. He was truthful *and* loving.

JESUS AND THE WEE LITTLE MAN

Consider his encounter with Zacchaeus (Luke 19:1–10). Jesus is passing through the small village of Jericho on a warm spring day, and everyone is outside. They see Jesus coming and they swarm the road. Jesus stops, scans the crowd, and then looks up into a nearby tree and sees a man perched on a branch trying to lay eyes on him. Come to find out, this man was a chief tax collector. And he was hated by everyone else.

During Jesus's time, tax collectors were Jews who worked for the Roman Empire—the dark side of the first-century force. Rome had conquered and occupied Israel through much war and bloodshed. They became the oppressive overlords who ruled the land. If you live in America, it's hard to picture this—unless you're Native American. We haven't had anyone invade our country and take it over. But imagine that North Korea, or Iran, or some other country conquered America and ruled the land. They parachuted into your city, took your stuff, and told you what to do and what not to do. And there was nothing you could say about it. Then imagine that your next-door neighbor went to work for this foreign country. He now goes door-to-door to take people's money and give it to your new rulers.

That's Zacchaeus. He's a Jew who's collecting taxes from his own people and giving them to Rome. Ancient tax collectors were committing political and religious *treason*. They turned their back on their country and on God, and they went to work for the enemy. Plus, they were known for living excessively immoral lives. They committed extortion, exhibited greed, and were usually immoral in every possible way.

And there stands Jesus. Gazing up into the tree. And he notices a tax collector. But not just any tax collector. Zacchaeus was a *chief* tax collector and he was *rich*. Not only was he an extortionist—he must have been a very successful one!

What would you expect Jesus to say? He could have called Zacchaeus on the carpet and shamed him in front of the crowd. "Come here, you little jerk! How dare you cheat and steal and lie. You'd better give back everything that you stole or I'm going to go all messianic on you!" Jesus could have rubbed Zacchaeus's face in his many sins. He could have confronted. He could have shouted. He could have grabbed him by the ankles, turned him upside down— Zacchaeus being a wee little man and all—and emptied his pockets of all his stolen money. But what does Jesus say?

"Zacchaeus, come down at once. I must stay at your house today." (Luke 19:5)

That's it. No confrontation. No rebuke. No shame. No MMA moves. Nothing.

It's fascinating that Jesus says, "I must stay at your house today." Jesus wasn't just looking for shelter. He was looking for friendship. In Jesus's day, staying at someone's house meant that you were friends with that person. That you valued that person. That you cared for the person and enjoyed being around them. Only friends would stay at each other's house. Enemies wouldn't cross the threshold of another enemy's house.

But Jesus isn't Zacchaeus's enemy. He's his friend.

After Jesus enters Zacchaeus's house, the crowd goes nuts! "Jesus has gone to be the guest of a sinner,'" they whisper. But Jesus goes anyway. He cares more about welcoming a sinner than pleasing the religious crowds. Once he's inside the house, you might expect Jesus to shut the door, turn to Zacchaeus, and say: "Okay, look. I didn't want to do this in front of everyone. But you've got some *serious issues*. You're a liar, a cheater, a thief, and an abomination before God. If you don't repent, you're going to hell!" But Jesus doesn't say this.

What does Jesus say?

Nothing.

He doesn't say a word.

He doesn't talk to Zacchaeus about his stance on extortion, nor does he march through the laundry list of Zacchaeus's sins. Jesus doesn't confront, nor does he rebuke. He simply accepts and loves.

Now look at Zacchaeus's response:

Zacchaeus stood up. He said, "Look, Lord! Here and now I give half of what I own to those who are poor. And if I have cheated anybody out of anything, I will pay it back. I will pay back four times the amount I took." (Luke 19:8)

In other words, Zacchaeus repents. He turns from his sin. He desires to be holy. He wants to change his lifestyle. And it wasn't Jesus's "stance on extortion" that motivated Zacchaeus's repentance. Rather, it was Zacchaeus's encounter with the unconditional acceptance of Christ.

Here's the main point I want us to get. *Sinners in need of grace can't obey God until they know that they are first accepted by God. Acceptance precedes obedience.*

JESUS FRONTS LOVE

When Jesus met Zacchaeus—a horrible sinner—he fronted love. And this is the same pattern we see throughout Jesus's life. Whenever he meets with people whom religious people thought were terrible sinners, Jesus fronts love. Check it out.

When Jesus meets a military leader of Rome—that oppressive empire ruling over Israel—he fronts love. He could have destroyed his enemy, and all the religious people would have cheered him on. But instead, Jesus conquered the military leader with love. When he asked Jesus to heal his servant, Jesus responds not with a sword but with grace (Matthew 8:5–12).

The same goes for Matthew, another tax collector like Zacchaeus (Matthew 9:9–13). Jesus sees "a man named Matthew sitting at the tax collector's booth" and says to him: "Follow me." Immediately, "Matthew got up and followed him" (Matthew 9:9). Just like his encounter with Zacchaeus, Jesus accepts Matthew without lecturing him about his stance on tax collecting.

We see the same pattern every time Jesus meets "sinners." In the story of the prodigal son, the father who represents God "felt compassion, and ran and embraced" his sinful son *before* he knew that his son was repentant (Luke 15:20 ESV). Jesus declared to the woman caught in adultery, "Neither do I condemn you," *before* he said, "go and sin no more" (John 8:11 NKJV). Jesus forgave the many sins of a prostitute who was washing his feet without ever mentioning her sins (Luke 7:36–50).

Does this mean that Jesus affirmed everyone's sin? Of course not. Did Jesus care about obedience? Absolutely. Did Jesus care about truth? (Do I really need to answer this?) Whenever Jesus encounters people who were engaged in sin, Jesus fronted love. He loved people *into* obedience. After all, it's God's kindness that leads to repentance, not our repentance that leads to God's kindness (Romans 2:4).

GAY IS THE NEW TAX COLLECTOR

Even though Jesus never mentions homosexuality, in many ways Christians have treated LGBT people the same way that ancient religious Jews treated tax collectors. And so Jesus's approach to tax collectors gives us a good model for how we are to relate to the LGBT community around us.

We have to be careful with this analogy though. Gay people are actually nothing like tax collectors of the first century, so I'm not comparing LGBT people to tax collectors. I'm only comparing how religious people *have viewed* the two. Ancient Jewish people treated tax collectors with scorn, ridicule, and shame. And many Christians have treated LGBT people the same: with scorn, ridicule, and shame.

But then there's Jesus—full of truth *and* love. Perfectly loving and perfectly truthful. Remember: Jesus has a very high ethical standard and deeply desires our obedience. But we have to ask the question: Why does Zacchaeus obey?

He obeys because he first was accepted.

Certainly Jesus didn't approve of Zacchaeus's sinful life, and yet he didn't feel the need to address every sin in his life. "You know, Zacchaeus, we can be friends and all, but you first have to know where I stand on the issue of extortion. And I guess I'll stay at your house, but first you need to give back all the money you stole." Jesus doesn't do that. Even though he desires Zacchaeus's obedience, he knows that the only way he'll get that obedience is by first showing acceptance.

Christians have often done a terrible job of accepting gay people. Maybe it's because we've thought that if we show acceptance, then this will look like we affirm same-sex relations. We've been scared about the message this might send.

But was Jesus worried that his acceptance would mean that he approved of Zacchaeus's treason?

I don't think Jesus cared too much about his reputation. He only cared about loving sinners like crazy—*especially* the ones the religious people had a hard time accepting. In fact, Jesus had so many friends who were drunks and tax collectors and partiers that he developed his own reputation: "This fellow is always eating and drinking far too much," the religious people said of Jesus. "He's a friend of tax collectors and 'sinners'" (Matthew 11:19).

Until Christians develop the reputation of being far too chummy with the LGBT community, we fail to imitate Christ.

Acceptance doesn't equal *affirmation*. That is, accepting someone's humanity doesn't mean that you approve of everything they do. Therefore, you should be eager to accept gay and lesbian people *as people*, and this doesn't mean that you applaud their every act.

JESUS LOVE

But many people today don't agree. They think that you can't love someone unless you affirm everything they do. Have you ever run into this? If you try to help someone to stop sinning, or if you disagree with something they're doing, they turn around and say, "I thought you loved me." This is pretty normal in the world's way of thinking. The assumption is that if you truly love someone, you will let them live however they want.

But this isn't biblical love. This isn't *Jesus*-like love. Biblical love isn't *based on* a person's holiness—if you do the right thing then I'll love you. But it does *seek* a person's holiness. Jesus said, "If you love me, keep my commandments." But he didn't say, "If you keep my commandments, *then* I will love you."

Biblical love is unconditional. But that doesn't mean that such love doesn't care about obedience. I think this is why so many Christians are scared to love LGBT people too much. They fear that if they "accept" them, this means they "affirm" homosexual behavior. But Jesus never had this fear and neither should we. Again, *acceptance doesn't mean affirmation.* Think about it.

Jesus hung out with prostitutes, but he didn't endorse prostitution.

Jesus hung out with tax collectors, but he didn't affirm extortion.

Jesus became friends with a woman caught in adultery, but he wasn't pro-adultery.

Acceptance doesn't have to mean affirmation. Biblical love *accepts* people as they are, and then loves them into the people God wants them to be.

GAY PEOPLE IN THE CHURCH

The fact is, most gay people I know who grew up in the church ended up leaving the church *not* because of the church's stance against homosexual *behavior*, but because of its stance against gay *people*. Listen to the testimony of just a few.

- Eric Borges was raised in a Christian home but experienced same-sex attraction. And he was ridiculed at school. "My name was not Eric, but Faggot. I was stalked, spit on, and ostracized . . . I was told that the inherent, very essence of my being was unacceptable." Even his Christian parents told him he was "disgusting, perverted, unnatural, and damned to hell."[1]

- Ben Wood was a Christian teen who was active in his youth group. He also struggled with same-sex attraction. One day at youth group, his youth pastor shamed him in front of the entire group: "You all know . . . that Ben is gay. Who here is comfortable being around him?" Then, "Do you understand that Ben is going to hell?" Ben was then told that he could not attend the upcoming mission trip and that he didn't deserve to be part of the youth group. Ben was shamed, humiliated, and betrayed by other kids in the group who were pressured into agreeing with the youth pastor.[2]

- You've already met my friend Lesli. She was a transgender youth who was trying to follow Jesus. But when she was told that she was an "abomination," "un-savable," and "damned to hell," she left the

---

1   See Eric's testimony on YouTube, which was posted one month before he killed himself; www.youtube.com/watch?v=0WymBCOSB_c

2   www.um-insight.net/in-the-church/mother%27s-video-captures-online-attention/

church and the faith. *"I was ashamed that I was such an abomination to the God that I adored."*

- Tim Otto is attracted to the same sex and grew up as a missionary kid. He often struggled with his faith and sexuality—and still does. One night, Tim had sex with an anonymous man in the back room of an adult bookstore. Immediately after, he contemplated suicide. As he recalls: "I wish that somehow, rather than ending up in the arms of that anonymous man, I could have found myself in the arms of the church . . . I wish in the church I had found myself loved."[3]

Fortunately, Tim didn't commit suicide that night. Shortly after, he found the love he was looking for—the love of other Christians who accepted him. Most of them didn't approve of homosexual behavior (and neither did Tim), but they accepted Tim for who he was and helped him with his struggles.

Likewise, Lesli was welcomed back into the church by a loving pastor who treated her like a human and not an abomination. This pastor believes that same-sex relations are sinful, but he also believes—as Jesus showed—that *not* loving same-sex *people* is sinful as well. Lesli is now a wonderful believer in Jesus.

Unfortunately, not every story ends on a positive note. One month after Eric Borges told his story through a YouTube video, he killed himself. Ben Wood also couldn't handle the loneliness and shame any longer. A few years after he was shamed in front of the youth group, he also killed himself.

---

3   Ibid., 6.

Many same-sex-attracted teens end up committing suicide. The statistics are staggering, *especially* for teens who grew up in the church. And like the testimonies above, these teens didn't kill themselves because they were told that same-sex *behavior* is wrong. Rather, they were mocked, ridiculed, dehumanized, unwanted, and unloved. And there's nothing Christlike about this. Jesus attracted many tax collectors and sinners to himself (Luke 15:1), but they didn't walk about wanting to kill themselves. Why is it that same-sex-attracted teens want to shove a gun between their teeth after encountering Christians?

We need to be more like Jesus.

You can be different. You can be both *truthful* and *loving* just like Jesus was. Being truthful means that we believe what God says about homosexual behavior. Being loving means we accept people for who they are and love them into obedience. *Acceptance precedes obedience.*

WHEN TWO LESBIANS WALK INTO YOUR CHURCH

I read a story a while back about two lesbians who decided to go to church one Sunday just to make Christians mad.[4] "Let's just go for fun! We'll see how much we can push their buttons," Amy told her girlfriend. "I hear their motto is

---

4   John Burke, "When Two Lesbians Walk into a Church Seeking Trouble," *Charisma News*, March 13, 2014, www.charismanews.com/opinion/43109-when-two-lesbians-walk-into-a-church-seeking-trouble

'Come as you are,'" Amy scoffed. "I just want to prove that this means 'come as you are . . . unless you're gay.'"

So Amy and her girlfriend went to church. Not to learn, but to provoke. They flirted in front of everyone, held hands, and made it very clear that they were lesbians. How did the church respond?

Amy recalls: "Instead of the disgusted looks of contempt we expected, people met eyes with us and treated us like real people." It's pretty cool how this church fronted love. But there's something Amy says here that makes my heart break.

Expected.

"Instead of the disgusted looks of contempt we expected," they "treated us like real people." Amy and her girlfriend were shocked that these Christians treated them like real human beings and not monsters.

Why was this shocking? What else would they expect from a bunch of sinners saved by grace? How else should beggars who have found bread treat other beggars in search of bread?

"Expected." They expected Christians to treat them like abominations, monsters, a subspecies of the human race. Instead, they were shocked that followers of Christ actually acted like Christ.

But Amy's story has a happy ending. She ended up breaking up with her girlfriend, but she kept coming back to church. The more she was accepted, the more she returned, and the more she returned, the more she was accepted.

The more I listened and learned about the teachings of Jesus, the more I started to actually believe that God really did love me. I heard more and more about being His masterpiece, and in time, I actually started to believe it. The more I believed God actually could see something of value in me, the more I trusted Him.

Amy was accepted and loved. Unconditionally. And *that's why* she turned to God. Always remember: *Acceptance precedes obedience.* We can never obey God until we are first accepted by God. And we'll never experience acceptance by God until we are accepted by God's people.

CHAPTER SIX

I THINK I MIGHT BE GAY

INTRODUCTION

In our conversation so far, we've been focusing on how straight people should think about homosexuality. One reason for this is that most of the population doesn't personally wrestle with same-sex attraction. But since about 5 percent of the world experiences some level of same-sex attraction, one out of every twenty of you reading this are probably attracted to the same sex.[1] And maybe you've felt like an outsider so far. So I want to make sure you feel welcome to the group. Again, this book isn't an "us" versus "them" conversation. It's just a conversation about "us"—all of us who are sinners in need of God's grace.

So I want to talk with those of you who are wrestling with same-sex attraction. Maybe it's only a mild attraction, or maybe it's very strong. Maybe you're attracted to both guys and girls, or maybe you're exclusively attracted to the same gender. Some of you are still "in the closet" and haven't told anyone yet. Or perhaps you have and it didn't go so well.

---

1   Many surveys and studies have been done to determine how many people are attracted to the same sex, and the results have been very different. Some are as low as 1 percent while others are as high as 10 percent. As you can imagine, it's difficult to get an accurate survey of the entire population, so I've simply given a percentage that splits the difference between the two extremes.

Now, for those of us who aren't same-sex attracted, I want you to keep listening. You may feel like you're listening in on a conversation that isn't meant for you. But hey, those who experience same-sex attraction know how you feel! They often feel like they're listening in on a conversation that isn't meant for them. Plus, it'll be good for straight people to hear what I have to say. So let's keep going in our conversation.

If you're attracted to the same sex, let me first say that I deeply care for you. I know, I don't know you personally, and you don't know me personally. But I've known a lot of people who are attracted to the same sex and I'm truly moved by their pain and struggle, their joy and fear, their unique stories about how they have found hope in times of loneliness, and happiness in the midst of suffering. And how they have been extremely hurt by other people. And I want you to know that I'm not trying to write some book at you. I don't know your name, or the details of your personal story, but I want to keep having a conversation with you. You're not just a reader; you're a real person. Loved by God.

If you experience same-sex attraction, here are several things I want you to think about.

You are not an abomination.

I really hope you aren't struggling to believe this. I would love to know that you've never felt disgusting or shamed because you're attracted to the same sex. And I especially hope others haven't made you feel this way. But there's a good chance they have. I'm truly sorry for this. But there's one thing you need to know; no matter how you have felt about yourself, or how others have made you feel, *God* doesn't think of you as an abomination, creepy, weird, or disgusting.

God delights in you. He cherishes you. You are his masterpiece—a beautiful work of art. God doesn't just love you. He actually *likes you.* He created you, enjoys you, and identifies with your sorrow and pain. When you are lonely, he is there. When you are happy, he's happy too. When you look at yourself in the mirror and get angry or depressed or feel ashamed—God only sees a stunning work of art.

It's true that God considers all sexual immorality to be sin. This includes lust, pornography, sex outside of marriage, and same-sex intercourse. Which means we're all in the same boat! And it's also true that same-sex intercourse is called an "abomination" in Leviticus 18:22. But this verse is referring to the *act*, not the *person.* Gay *sex* is called an abomination, but gay *people* never are. They are created in God's image and are the object of his delight.

Same-sex attraction is not a sin.

As we've talked through earlier in this book, same-sex *attraction* is not the same as same-sex *behavior* (lust or sexual activity). It's important to realize that while same-sex behavior is sin, same-sex attraction is not. Nowhere in the Bible does it say that same-sex attraction is a sin. It may be a *temptation* to sin, and if the attraction turns into lust, then it becomes sin. But the fact that you are attracted to the same sex is not in itself a sin.

Some people disagree with me. They say that same-sex attraction is itself sin. But the Bible never says this. In fact, look at what James says:

> Temptation comes from our own desires, which entice us and drag us away. These desires give birth to sinful actions. And when sin is allowed to grow, it gives birth to death. (James 1:14–15 NLT)

James says that desires may "give birth to sinful actions," but that means that desires are *not* "sinful actions." Think about it. A woman may give birth to a child, but this means that the woman is not the child. They're different. In the same way, desires may give birth to sin, but the desires themselves are not sin. Same-sex attraction is one of these desires. It could lead us to sin. But being same-sex attracted isn't itself sin.

In fact, I would say that your same-sex attraction can actually lead to many positive behaviors. Some of the most encouraging, loyal, loving friends I have happen to be gay. Many of these friends choose not to act on their same-sex attraction. But they're still "gay." And their same-sex attraction allows them to see the world in new light. They value friendships in a much richer way. They long for the return of Christ with great passion. They resonate with other people who have been marginalized and shamed by society—poor people, racial minorities, people with disabilities.

God didn't *create* their same-sex attraction. But he can use it to help shape them to be amazing people.

There is a difference between attraction, orientation, behavior, gay, and Gay.

Since we're talking about attraction, we should distinguish this from other terms we've been using. Here's a quick summary:

- *Same-sex attraction* refers to one's sexual attraction to people of the same sex. There is no one-size-fits-all way to measure this. For some people it's strong, for others it's mild.

- *Same-sex orientation* simply refers to a strong and more fixed level of same-sex attraction. *Same-sex attraction* and *same-sex orientation* are often used interchangeably.

- *Same-sex behavior* refers to sexual acts, which include lust, sexual activity, and sexual intercourse.

- *gay* (lowercase) is a description of one's same-sex orientation. Such a person may or may not engage in sexual behavior, but they use the term *gay* as an easy way to describe their experience of same-sex attraction.

- *Gay* (uppercase) refers to one's identity based on their attraction to the same sex.

Okay, you got all of that? I've tried to keep it simple so I don't drown you with a pool of information. But you probably have some questions. For instance, under "same-sex behavior," maybe you're wondering what type of activity qualifies as "sexual activity." This is a good question. It's a good question for both same-sex attracted and straight people. I'm not sure there's a black-and-white answer, but I think that a good measure is this: sexual activity is anything you wouldn't do with your brother or sister.

Generally, people engage in three different types of relationships: family, friends, and romantic/sexual partners. You may kiss your mom on the cheek or hold hands with your sister. But this same act is going to mean something else if you do it with someone you are romantically attracted to.

This may sound harsh, but I don't think you should engage in any activity that you wouldn't do with a family member. This doesn't mean you can't be affectionate. Again, family members are affectionate. But everyone knows the difference between kissing your mom and kissing a hot boy or girl.

Sexual passion is one of the most powerful things we possess. If we don't master it, it'll master us.

Going back to our phrases, it's important to know that just because you're same-sex attracted doesn't mean you have to call yourself "gay." The word *gay*, or *Gay*, is a word some people use to describe themselves. But others don't. Not every same-sex-attracted person calls him- or herself gay. It's an identity label. And not everyone wants to identify themselves by their sexual attraction.

If you choose to describe yourself as gay, I would recommend that you only use the term to describe your attractions. I don't feel it's good for Christians to label themselves as "Gay" (uppercase) as their primary identity. Our identity is in

Christ—everything else is secondary. We are first and foremost followers of the risen Jesus. And we don't want anything to muffle our primary identity. There's a lot of terms I can use to describe myself: man, father, husband, professor, writer, Netflix connoisseur. But these are all secondary descriptions of myself; my primary identity is "I'm a Christian."

You're not alone.

Most of my gay friends tell me that when they first wrestled with their same-sex attraction, they felt so alone. All the other guys were slobbering over girls. And all the other girls were gazing at the guys. Every conversation with their friends centered on which guy or girl they liked. And it wasn't long before they felt like they were the only person on the planet who felt differently. So they tried to go along with the conversations, just to fit in.

Maybe you've felt this way. Maybe you've tried to date someone of the opposite sex just to show that you're just like everyone else. But deep down, you know. You know you're different. And you think you're the only one.

But you need to know that you're not. Again, around 5 percent of the planet experiences some level of same-sex attraction. However, many of them don't tell anyone. There's a good chance that several people at your church are attracted to the same sex and yet nobody knows about it. Stay-at-home moms, youth group leaders, elders, deacons, grandparents whom you thought were no longer attracted to anyone. You're not alone, even if you still feel that way after reading this paragraph.

Or maybe you've come out to your friends and family, but now everything is just weird. They don't know what to do with you. They don't know what to say or how to act, and you get the sense that they would rather be anywhere other than in your presence. But trust me: There are others who feel just like you do. You're not the only one going through what you're experiencing.

This leads us to the next point.

Find someone to talk to.

Some of you have already found someone to talk to. If that someone is authentic, loving, wise, and understanding, then consider yourself blessed. In fact, make sure you thank this person for being a listening ear and loving friend. Such people are rare.

Even if you have found someone who is there for you, I would try to find a few more. You don't need to spill your guts to everyone you meet. But you do need to find a loving and honest community of people whom you can lean on. Several of my gay friends have found such communities, and they tell me that it's the most life-giving thing on earth. Others have not found such communities, and they are very lonely.

God hasn't wired us to figure stuff out on our own. We all need relationships. We all need love. We need a community of believers who can "take on the shape of our pain," as Bono says.[2]

---

2   "Troubles," in *Songs of Innocence*.

If you haven't told anyone about your attraction, then pray that God would lead you to the right person. I don't think you should come out to just anyone. And you need to do it when you're ready. But it's something I strongly feel you should do. You can't sort through all of this by yourself. It won't work. You won't be able to handle it.

I realize that some of you may not have anyone who will understand what you're going through. You're pretty sure they would flip out if you told them. I get this. I have a friend back east who's same-sex attracted, and he goes to a very conservative church. He says that he could never tell people at his church about his attraction. They would all freak out!

If this is you, then you still need to find someone to talk to. Maybe it's a pastor of another church. Maybe it's a professor, or a friend's parent, or someone you have come to know well and trust online. Heck, you can Facebook me and we can get to know each other if you want! I'm all ears. Or all eyes, I guess. Either way, pray that God would lead you to the right person. You weren't meant to handle this on your own.

Give grace to your parents and friends.

Many of you who have come out have not received the best welcome. It's very common for friends or parents—especially parents—to react in really weird and obnoxious ways when their loved one tells them they're attracted to the same sex. Perhaps your parents said things like:

- "How could you do this to us!"

- "When did you choose this?"

- "What about that girl you took to the prom?"

- "You're a Christian. You can't be gay!"

Or the worst one: "Oh . . . uh . . . that's nice, honey. Uh . . . What do you want for dinner?" Blissful denial. Sometimes it's the only way parents can cope.

You've got to give your parents and friends some grace. For most of them, they simply don't know what to say or how to react. They don't realize how painful or ignorant their responses can be.

Hopefully some of you have had good responses from your loved ones. People are becoming more and more understanding of same-sex-attracted people. I'll never forget when one of my college students came out in front of three thousand classmates at a chapel service. It was "student testimony" day, where students went to the mic and told everyone what God had been doing in their lives. A student named Zach got up, walked over to the mic, took out a piece of paper, and started reading his testimony in front of those three thousand people. He went into detail about how he was attracted to guys and lived as a gay teen in a gay community for several years before coming to college. But he recently found Christ and was trying to be faithful to him. After he finished, you could have heard a pin drop. A wave of sweat immediately covered his flesh. But seconds later, he was mobbed by a group of guys with hugs, high fives, fist bumps, and authentic affirmations that Zach was loved.

There wasn't a dry eye in the chapel. It was a beautiful, Zacchaeus-like moment.

But for those of you who haven't experienced such a welcome, be patient with your loved ones. Forgive them for all the stupid things they've said or the horrible ways they treated your coming out. If you hold on to your bitterness or frustration, it'll only eat you up from the inside out. Let it go. Forgive them in the same way that God has forgiven you.

Accept God's forgiveness.

Speaking of which, make sure *you* accept God's forgiveness for any sin you've committed. If you haven't acted on your attraction, then this doesn't apply to you in this case. But if you have engaged in same-sex behavior, or have entertained lustful thoughts, you may have a hard time accepting God's forgiveness.

You need to know that God doesn't forgive people begrudgingly. He dishes it out generously. There are no appetizers in God's banquet room. Only huge, luscious portions of forgiveness for us to feast on. God isn't just capable of forgiving you; he delights in wiping away your sin, never to be remembered again.

Think about the death of Christ. Was it powerful enough to forgive your sin? Did Jesus really pay the penalty? Did he truly remove all our guilt and shame?

Yes, of course he did. He took it all—100 percent. Jesus didn't cover 90 percent of our sin, leaving us to beat ourselves up over the other 10 percent. He took every sin—past, present, and future—and slammed it into a grave. And when he walked out, he left our sin there. We are forgiven. We are cleared of all our guilt.

So when you hang on to your sin and refuse to accept God's forgiveness, you're basically telling God that the death of his son was not enough. "Thanks, God, for helping me out, but I need to take it from here."

Some of you have sinned. Like, the really bad stuff. You've lusted after other people. You've had sex with anonymous guys or have some secret thing going on with another girl. Whatever the case may be, if you truly love God, and desire to be faithful to him, then when you mess up, God is eager to forgive. This doesn't mean that he gives you a license to sin. Don't take sin lightly. It'll destroy you. But so will trying to cover your own sin by bearing the guilt.

You've been freed. You've been forgiven. And you are loved. Believe it!

Banish the thought of suicide.

The final thing I want to say is that suicide is not an option. Don't do it. Don't even think about it. It's frighteningly common for gay teens to take their lives. In fact, 41 percent of all transgender people and 20 percent of gay or lesbian individuals have attempted suicide. Compare this to 4.6 percent of the US population as a whole.[3]

So if you've contemplated it, or even attempted it, please banish the thought of ever doing it again. If you've thought about it, then you must have some really deep pain and loneliness in your heart. And I'm incredibly sorry that you

---

3   Ann P. Haas et. al., *Suicide Attempts Among Transgender, and Gender Non-Conforming, Adults*, January 2014, http://williamsinstitute.law.ucla.edu/wp-content/uploads/AFSP-Williams-Suicide-Report-Final.pdf

are going through what you are. Depression and loneliness are terrible things; they are the Devil's strongest weapons against us. In no way do I belittle your real pain and suffering. And if you live near Boise, Idaho, then let's grab some coffee and talk about it. I would love to hear your story and help out in any way. And I'm sure there is someone near you who would say the same. Pray for that person to come into your life. Suicide is not the solution and it's never the right thing to do.

After all, God created you not just to *be* loved, but *to* love. People need you. They will be blessed by you. If you take your life, you're not allowing God to use you to love and serve other people. God gave you life. It's not yours to take.

I'm serious. Please Facebook me or Tweet me (@PrestonSprinkle) if you have no one to talk to. We can swap numbers and go from there.

CHAPTER SEVEN

MY BEST FRIEND IS GAY . . . NOW WHAT?

INTRODUCTION

Now, let's all come back together and regroup. I want to talk to those of you who have friends or family who are gay, or same-sex attracted (SSA). I'm going to use the term *gay* interchangeably with SSA from here on out. Even if you don't know anyone who is LGBT—or don't *yet* know that someone in your life is—there's a good chance you will get to know someone in the near future. Some of what I'm going to say will relate to what we talked about in the previous chapter. Only now, we're talking about those of us who are trying to respond with love and truth to our friends or family who are LGBT.

Shortly before I wrote this book, there was a story that made international headlines. Perhaps you remember when Leelah Alcorn committed suicide in December 2014 and posted a suicide note on her blog just hours before her death. The note was painful to read. But it also can help us all do a better job relating to LGBT people who are dealing with deep emotional pain.

Leelah, whose birth name was Joshua, was a transgender youth. She felt like a girl trapped in a boy's body. (I'll keep calling Leelah "she" since that's how she described herself.) She was also raised in a conservative Christian home. Leelah, though biologically male, felt like a female ever since she was four years old. She was confused, tormented, and didn't know what to do. But when she was fourteen years old, she discovered the word *transgender*, and finally it all made sense. The next thing she did was tell her mother—this is what she says in her suicide note:

> I immediately told my mom, and she reacted extremely negatively, telling me that it was a phase, that I would never truly be a girl, that God doesn't make mistakes, that I am wrong.

What do you think? Is this a good response? What do you think Leelah's mom should have said? I should add that her mom was terribly grieved over Leelah's death and said that she loved her child unconditionally. I don't think her mom was at all malicious in her response. But here's how Leelah goes on to describe her reaction:

> If you are reading this, parents, please don't tell this to your kids. Even if you are Christian or are against trans-gender people don't ever say that to someone, especially your kid. That won't do anything but make them hate them self. That's exactly what it did to me.[1]

Even if you have good intentions, what you say to

---

1   The suicide note was taken down, but a copy of it can be found here: Michael Stone, "Transgender Teen Commits Suicide, Cites Christian Parents in Blog," *Progressive Secular Humanist*, December 29, 2014, www.patheos.com/blogs/progressivesecularhumanist/2014/12/transgender-teen-commits-suicide-cites-christian-parents-in-blog/#ixzz3RUJtAx6O

someone can have tremendous power. Words can heal or hurt; they can tear down or build up. Words alone don't cause someone to commit suicide. But they sometimes play a role. Even unintentionally. This is why it's so important that we learn how to respond in truth and love to our friends or family who come out. Here are a few ways to do this.

Listen, and don't react.

This is by far the most important thing you can do. Just listen. To listen is to love; you can't truly love unless you first listen. This applies to every type of relationship, actually. Deep, loving relationships are built upon mutual listening. Have you ever been in a conversation where you are pouring your heart out and the other person doesn't even look you in the eye? They're sitting in your presence, but they're not really there. You're saying things you feel are really important, and your friend is like, "Yeah . . . uh-huh . . . uh-huh . . . ummm . . . Hey, check out this cool YouTube video I just found!" Isn't this frustrating? Doesn't it feel so unloving?

Now what about the times when you are sharing something deeply personal? And the person you're talking to just stares into your eyes and listens. Their eyes aren't darting around the room. They're not checking their phone. They aren't cutting you off midsentence. They just listen.

You can't love someone unless you listen. And this is by far the most important thing my LGBT friends have told me. When they came out—which is a frightening thing to do—their parents or friends didn't listen. They just reacted: "What! You can't be gay. You've had several girlfriends!" Or "God says that homosexuality is a sin; you need to stop being gay." Even questions like the ones we mentioned in the last chapter aren't real questions: "When did you choose this?" Or "What about that boy who took you to the prom?" These aren't real questions. They're accusations with a question mark.

There will be time for you to talk, but not until you listen. If you want to ask questions, ask *real* questions, like: "How did you feel when you first realized you were attracted to boys (or girls)?" and "How can I be a friend to you right now?"

Bottom line: Don't react. Even if your friend is angry, obnoxious, or even offensive. Maybe they're cussing up a storm, or yelling at you. Let it go. Psychologists say that deep pain often produces stronger statements. It's sort of a coping mechanism, a way of dealing with stuff going on inside. So look past the reaction and get to the heart. Let them vent, let them cry, let them be real with what's going on inside. It's the only way you'll get to what's *going on inside*.

Listen. Learn. And love. It's the only way you'll be able to be a friend to the person opening up to you.

Express your commitment to them.

When it is time for you to talk, the most effective thing you can do is express your commitment to your friend. That is, if you truly desire to be committed. Don't blow smoke up their nose. They know when you're being real and when you don't really mean what you say. But if you truly desire to stay committed to your friend—and as a follower of Jesus, you should!—then that needs to be the first thing out of your mouth. Or if you have a friend who has already told you that she's gay, and you haven't expressed your commitment, then it's never too late. Let them know you are there for them and you will always be there for them—no matter what.

Now let's think back to our conversation about *acceptance* versus *affirmation*. Jesus accepted *sinners* like Zacchaeus, even though he never affirmed *sin*. The same rule applies here. You can be unconditionally committed to someone, and even if they go their own way and end up living like the Devil, you can still be committed to the person even though you don't approve of their lifestyle.

I remember hearing an awesome story from Tullian Tchividjian, a famous preacher these days, who's also the grandson of Billy Graham. Tullian's not gay, but his story is a good example of feeling accepted without being affirmed. Tullian was raised in a Christian home but he was the black sheep of the family. He partied like crazy in high school and wanted nothing to do with Christianity.

One day, his father's friend sat him down and reamed him for his rebelliousness. "How dare you act like this! Do you know who your father is? You need to get your act together and stop living the way you are." All truth, but no love. And no acceptance.

Tullian recalls that he couldn't wait to get away from that guy.

Fast forward a year and Tullian is still living like the prodigal son. Another friend of his father's sits him down over lunch and says, "You know, Tullian, I really care for you and your family. And I know that you're going through a lot of stuff right now. I just want you to know that if you ever need anything or if you ever find yourself in trouble, I want you to call me. Day or night. I'll be here for you. Here's my number."

Tullian said that he didn't want him to leave! He just wanted to talk to the guy for hours and pour out his guts. Why? Because he felt accepted, even though he knew the man didn't affirm his life.

Make sure you reaffirm your unconditional commitment to your friend. Tell them that you'll be there for them. No matter what.

Know the difference between the terms *gay*, *attraction*, and *behavior*.

We already talked about this in the last chapter. So if you skipped over it, it'll be good to go back and read section 3 on page **87**. As we discussed, there's a difference between being gay, experiencing same-sex attraction, and engaging in same-sex behavior.

As you're listening to your friend, don't read too much into everything they say. They may say, "I'm gay," and all they mean is that they're attracted to the same sex. It doesn't necessarily mean they are acting on that attraction. Or they may say they are gay, but perhaps they are bisexual. Or maybe they've experienced some mild same-sex attraction and are just trying to figure things out.

Remember my friend Jordan, whom I told you about in chapter 1? He admitted that he was same-sex attracted and some people assumed that he was living a "gay lifestyle." But Jordan had never engaged in any form of sexual behavior. Therefore, he wasn't in sin.

Don't get me wrong. Your friend may mean exactly what they say. "I'm gay" might mean "I'm not just struggling with same-sex attraction, but I identify as gay." My point is that you need to make sure you understand what your friend means by the terms they are using. Again, it goes back to the whole listening thing.

Honor their parents.

Some of the worst experiences happen when a gay teen comes out to their parents. We saw this with Leelah, and I've heard even worse stories about parents flying off the handle. You can imagine the pain and confusion that many parents will have when they realize that their child is gay—especially if the parents are Christians. Oftentimes, parents will respond in offensive, demeaning, or unhelpful ways. But usually their intentions are good. In the same way that an SSA person my react rather strongly to cope with the pain, parents also may go nuts in the moment and say things they don't really mean.

So what's your role in all of this? If your friend tells you about the horrible ways they've been treated by their parents, what do you say? How do you react? These are tough waters to navigate.

On the one hand, you want to be there for your friend. Again, you want to listen, love, and show them that you're committed. You don't want to correct every little thing they say and do. You want to let them talk about how they feel—even if what they are feeling at that moment isn't always that good.

On the other hand, you don't want to fuel the fire of bitterness. Nor do you want to play an active role in gossip. At the end of the day, you want your friend to be able to forgive his parents, even if they have really wronged him and made him feel terrible. We all know it's hard to forgive people when they have really hurt us. It feels so good in the moment to hold on to anger and bitterness, to lash out with vengeful words and scathing thoughts. But this will only turn into emotional cancer. A bitter person is an unhappy person; a vengeful heart is a rotten heart. So while you want to listen to your friend and give them space to vent and authentically grieve, you also want to help them forgive and be healed.

Plus, unless you really know their parents and have seen their conversations, there's a chance that your friend could be misrepresenting them. We've all done this, right? Our parents tell us something we don't like. And after we let it simmer for a few hours, we relate the conversation to our friends in a way that makes our parents look much worse than they are.

I'm not saying that your friend will always misrepresent his parents. I'm only saying that it's a possibility. Either way, you want to balance being supportive without not adding fuel to the fire.

Don't assume that your friend is sexually attracted to you.

This is a common fear among straight folks. We think that if we get too close to our gay friends (of the same gender), they'll fall in love with us. I used to think this until I started befriending gay people, and they all said that they crave same-gender friendships. They also say that it's not very common that they fall in love with their straight friends. I'm not saying it doesn't happen. Certainly it does. But it's not as common as you think. After all, if they know you're straight and they know you're trying to be a good friend, it would be a serious breach of trust for them to make a move on you and ruin a good friendship.

There's still a risk, of course, that they may secretly fall in love with you and not act on it. (Just like what can sometimes happen in male-female friendships.) But I would recommend taking that risk. All relationships run the risk of ending in pain or confusion. I've never met a person who doesn't have some story about having a relationship that blew up in their face. Maybe it was jealousy, or perhaps lack of forgiveness. Some people have such a hard time letting go of even the smallest offense. You forgot to call, or you didn't invite them to the movies last week. Even though you apologize and feel bad for letting them down, they can't let it go. Friendship dead.

This side of heaven, sin will always try to ruin good relationships, but this doesn't mean we don't pursue relationships. The same is true of continuing a relationship with our gay friends. There's a (small) risk that their attraction could mess with a good friendship. But a good friendship is worth the risk.

And as always, if this is a real fear of yours, it might be good to talk to them about it. You've got to be careful, though. You don't want to make it sound like they're wanting to have sex with every same-gender person they meet.

That's another horrible stereotype about gay people: that being gay means you want to have lots and lots of gay sex. Anyway, if you have any of these fears or questions, just talk to your friend about them. Admit your ignorance. Show your heart in wanting to know. And as always: *Listen, listen, listen!*

If you think your friend might be gay . . .

Now here's a tough one. Maybe you have a friend who hasn't come out, but it seems like she's gay. We all know the stereotypes. Tomboy girls who love the ball field more than the mall. Artsy boys who . . . well . . . love the mall more than the ball field. What should you do?

The first thing you should do is avoid gender stereotypes. I've known feminine-looking men who talk with a lisp who are raging heterosexuals. I've also known gay men who bench-press three hundred pounds and can throw a football farther than Tom Brady. Our culture, and oftentimes our church, has done us a huge disfavor by spoon-feeding us a one-size-fits-all view of what it means to be a man or a woman. As I said earlier, I believe God wants girls to act like girls, and boys to act like boys. *But what it means to act like a boy or girl is rather flexible.* Not every straight boy needs to be athletic and outdoorsy, and not every girl needs to love dresses and makeup. These are stereotypes. They do not capture the beautiful diversity of actual people. So make sure you don't base your assumption about someone's orientation on some stereotype of maleness and femaleness.

Anyway, back to our question. If you think one of your friends might be gay, what should you do?

First, avoid direct questions like, "Hey, so, are you gay?" This could not only be offensive, it could also crush someone who really isn't gay. Or maybe they *have been* struggling with same-sex attraction, and now you may have unintentionally confirmed that they really must be gay. This could (mis)lead them down a path they shouldn't take. Or it could force them to "come out" when they weren't prepared to do so.

On that note, second, it's always best for the person to come out of the closet and not be dragged out of it. You can help them come out. But they must take the first steps.

Third, be a good friend to them without asking if they are gay. If they really do struggle with same-sex attraction, and you really do care about them (and not just care to know whether they're gay or not), then become a better friend. Get to know them. Build some trust. Share with them some of your own struggles. If they really are same-sex attracted, then they'll want to confide in someone whom they can trust. Maybe that someone will be you.

Believe that sexual sin is destructive.

We've been emphasizing *love* for the past couple chapters. So let me end by circling back around to the importance of truth. Plain and simple: Sexual sin is destructive. Period.

Notice I didn't single out *same-sex* sexual sin. That's destructive too. But so is heterosexual pornography, sex outside of marriage, and mild forms of sexual activity outside of marriage that almost always lead to sex outside of marriage, which can lead to pregnancy, which can lead to single parenthood or adoption or abortion. There's nothing good and loving and healthy about sexual sin. It's deceptive. It's artificial, superficial, and will officially eat away at your humanity bit by bit.

Now, as we've seen, God has not designed us to have same-sex intercourse, even in the context of marriage. It's against God's will and it is sin. And sin is destructive. It's not good for us. Sin does not help humans to flourish; it prevents us from living out our humanity in the best possible way.

After all, God is not some cosmic killjoy who wants us to be miserable. God wants us to experience true happiness and joy. And *this is why* he gave us rules. Not to steal our joy, but to enhance it.

Sin is like a fishing hook and we are like fish. "Stay away from those extra-plumpy worms," our Fishmaster tells us. "They're not what you think." But we can't resist. He can't be right. *That fat little worm looks so darn tasty. It must be good for me."* And so we follow the worm. We examine it, trying to discover its deceit. We don't see any potential destruction. *It sure looks like it'll make me happy.* We then make excuses why the fat little worm will be good for us. And then we chomp, and munch, and enjoy a few moments of bliss. But then we feel a sharp pain knifing its way through our upper lip. And we wish we had left that fat little worm alone.

I know, it's a goofy example. But you get the point, right? *Sin may look good, but it's actually bad for us.* It's not just forbidden fun. It's a deadly deed. And since homosexual sex is sin, then no matter how much you think it'll make someone happy or fulfilled or help them flourish as a human, there's a hook inside that fat little worm.

As you're seeking to love your gay friends with truth, we need to help them believe that homosexual sex is destructive. I'm not saying this needs to be the first, second, or even tenth conversation. If your friend is a Christian, he or she probably knows it's sin. But sex is powerful, and Satan is powerful too. Together, they are seeking to destroy people with same-sex attraction by convincing them that same-sex behavior is the only way they will flourish as humans. But this is a destructive lie.

Be a loving friend, and stick close to your gay friends as they swim in the midst of hidden hooks.

CHAPTER EIGHT

HOMOSEXUALITY ALL AROUND ME

INTRODUCTION

The topic of homosexuality is all around us. It's in the news, TV shows, movies, political discussions, and, I'm guessing, has been the subject of quite a few conversations you've had with your friends. Especially your friends who aren't Christians. Have you had this conversation yet? Someone finds out that you're a Christian, and the first thing they want to know is how you feel about homosexuality. My guess is that you're not sure how to respond to that question. You may think homosexuality is wrong, but you're not quite sure why. Or you know that the person asking the question will think you might as well be a racist bigot if you say it's sin. After all, if two people love each other and they aren't hurting anyone, how can you say it's sin, right?

It's hard to know how to respond to our changing culture. It's especially tough to know what to say, how to say it, and when to say it. Sometimes it's good to speak up. Other times we should keep our mouths shut. In every case, though, we need to point people to Jesus. We can't let our stance on homosexuality become a distraction from our primary message about a risen Savior and King named Jesus.

So how do we do this? Let's start with our response to all the talk about homosexuality in politics and the media.

HOMOSEXUALITY IN POLITICS AND MEDIA

Homosexuality often comes up in political debates. When I started writing this book, gay marriage was legal in thirty-seven out of our fifty states. But by the time I was finished, the Supreme Court ruled that gay marriage was now legal in the entire country. Consider the fast pace at which the legalization of gay marriage has occured:

- Prior to 2008, gay marriage was legal in only one state: Massachusetts.

- Between 2008 and 2013, gay marriage became legal in fifteen additional states.

- From 2013 to early 2015, gay marriage became legal in twenty-one additional states, bringing the total to thirty-seven states.

- In June 2015, gay marriage became legal in all fifty states.

That means that from the time you were born, gay marriage has gone from being illegal throughout the United States to legal in all fifty states. Talk about a rapid shift in view!

The same is true in the media. Back in 1998, NBC aired *Will and Grace*, which was the first hit show that regularly portrayed gay characters. This was pretty risky for the '90s. But all throughout the 2000s, many shows have contained gay characters: *Modern Family, The New Normal, Grey's Anatomy, Scandal, The Good Wife, Revenge, Orange Is the New Black, Transparent,* and the list goes on and on. It would be very rare these days for a show to make it past a season or two without having at least one gay character appear.

So what are we to think about all of this? How should we respond?

With regard to gay marriage, many Christians responded as if they thought the sky was falling after the Supreme Court ruled in favor of same-sex marriage. These Christians think that the church must stand against the secular tidal wave rushing at us from our culture. And the main force behind the wave is the "gay agenda."

There may be a bit of truth to this. But only a bit.

It's true that homosexuality has become widely accepted in a short amount of time. Certainly, the unbelieving world is sending a message that homosexuality is fine. But why should this surprise us? I hate to state the obvious, but *it's the unbelieving world.* What else should we expect? I love what Paul says in 1 Corinthians 5:

> When I wrote to you before, I told you not to associate with people who indulge in sexual sin. But I wasn't talking about unbelievers who indulge in sexual sin, or are greedy, or cheat people, or worship idols. You would have to leave this world to avoid people like that . . . *It isn't my responsibility to judge outsiders.* (1 Corinthians 5:9–10, 12, NLT, emphasis mine)

Paul says it's not our responsibility to judge outsiders. When an unbeliever produces a TV show that showcases a gay couple, we aren't to pass judgment or sneer or get angry. It's just yet another reminder that people need Jesus. And they won't find him through our anger. They may find him, though, when we dish out huge portions of Zacchaeus-like grace to the undeserving. Because that's what Jesus did.

Plus, we can actually learn some things from the LGBT characters on TV. As we've seen, Christians have often gone about the homosexuality question all wrong. We've treated it as some issue to debate and get angry about, rather than people who need the love of Christ. Some of the TV shows, at least, help us see LGBT people as *real people*. I know, the people on TV are not real. They're actors. Obviously. But many of these actors portray real-life experiences that are reflected in the lives of real LGBT people. And some actually are, in real life, part of the LGBT community.

For instance, my wife and I got addicted to the show *The Good Wife* a few years back. In it, the main character (Alicia Florrick) has a brother (Owen) who is gay. He fits a mild stereotype of how a gay man should act, but it's not over the top. Most of all, he's portrayed as a sensitive, kindhearted, fun-loving, and often wise—yet real and vulnerable—gay guy. The TV show makes you like him. It's hard to get angry at a guy who is super caring and enjoyable. I sometimes get lost in the show and think, "Man, I'd like to hang out with Owen."

Isn't that a good thing? For a Christian to *want* to be around a person who needs Jesus? To admire and appreciate the humanity of a human?

Does Owen's character make me rethink what the Bible says about homosexuality? No. Not at all. But does it put flesh on how I think about the "issue" of homosexuality? Absolutely.

So I don't think Christians need to be angry or scared about the increasing number of LGBT people in the media. If anything, it could help us look at them as real people and not some "other."

Some Christians also grumble about "the gay agenda," although it's not always clear what they mean by that phrase. It's true that some LGBT people have an aggressive agenda to gain equal rights through marriage laws and workplace diversity codes. But many LGBT people I know don't have any agenda at all. For instance, I have a gay friend who used to be a worship leader at a large church in California, but he left the faith a few years ago when he realized he was gay. He ended up partnering with another man and now they both live in Hollywood and work in the film industry. I had coffee with him a couple years ago because I wanted to hear his story. And I asked him how he felt about the LGBT community that lives in Hollywood. (In case you don't know, Hollywood has a massive LGBT community.)

"Yeah, we don't really hang out with that community. They can be so obnoxious and selfish," he said.

I was shocked. At the time I thought being gay came with its own membership card to the "gay community," where everyone sits around figuring out how they can push their "gay agenda" on all of us straight people. I guess I was wrong. In any case, I mustered up the courage to ask, "So you wouldn't participate in the gay rights parade that comes through town?"

"No way," he said. "I don't really care about 'gaining my rights' or 'gay marriage.' It's fine if some people want that, but that's not us. We just want to live a simple life. We like to go to work, come home and eat dinner, and then maybe watch a little TV, and then go to bed. We're a pretty boring couple, actually."

So here's a gay man living with another gay man in the heart of the so-called "gay agenda," yet he himself has no agenda other than living a simple life.

Again, this doesn't mean that he's living a God-glorifying life. But I fear that he and his partner could be caught in the crossfire when angry Christians think that every single gay person alive has an agenda to demoralize society.

People need Jesus. He's the good news we're proclaiming. We never want some culture war about homosexuality to drown out our triumphant message of God's grace toward sinners.

HOMOSEXUALITY IN MY COMMUNITY

So what about the homosexuality that's all around us in our communities: our classrooms, neighborhoods, local hangouts, and places of work? Most of you are probably on a high school or college campus where LGBT people are common. You may have teachers who are gay, fellow classmates who are gay, counselors, administration, bosses, coworkers, friends, and family—any of whom could be LGBT. Or maybe you even know some straight people—at least you thought they were straight—who are sexually experimenting with people of the same sex, just to see what it's like. Maybe they're gay, maybe they're not. The whole thing can just be so confusing.

So what's your response?

First of all, don't freak out. There's nothing new under the sun. Christians have been living in the midst of non-Christian cultures for thousands of years, and yet God continues to build his kingdom and save unlikely people. So be turned off by sin. Resist wickedness. Be angry at evil. But don't be shocked by it. Again, as Paul said above, who are we to judge unbelievers?

In fact, when Paul was traveling the Mediterranean world, society was much, much worse than it is now. Same-sex relations were widely accepted—even among men who were married to women. It was typical for husbands to have sex with a male household slave or the neighbor's son just for a sexual adventure. The artwork and graffiti that painted the cities were way more graphic than even our filthiest billboards today. Graphic images of orgies and men having sex with boys were plastered on the walls of public buildings. Sometimes they even decorated household drinking pitchers. Imagine asking your mother to pass you the water during dinnertime. Yikes!

And then there were the Roman emperors—the leaders of the empire. All but one emperor had same-sex partners—and sometimes quite a few. In fact, Caesar Nero, who was the emperor during Paul's day, married two different men in public. For one of his weddings, he dressed up like a woman—veil and all.

Christianity was born out of a pagan society that makes Las Vegas look like Mayberry. (Sorry, you may have to google that one.) And yet the gospel did just fine. The thick darkness of the pagan Roman culture didn't snuff out the light of the gospel. Christians flourished in their faith and they led many people to Christ. Yes, even people who were engaging in all kinds of sexual sin.

So I don't care how bad your campus is. God's been here before. He's not shocked at anything. Jesus looks at the homosexuality all around you and yawns.

Don't be shocked. Don't think Satan is winning, or that you don't stand a chance against the tide of sin washing over your campus or workplace. Stand tall and triumphant—you're a child of the risen King.

Second, be thoughtful in how you answer the "what's your view on homosexuality" question. This question is usually the tip of a very large iceberg, especially when a gay person is asking it. Remember, most LGBT people have had a really bad experience with churches. Many of them have been shamed and dehumanized—unloved to say the least! So if you just give a quick answer, like "I think homosexuality is sin," there's a good chance they'll interpret that as "You think I'm an abomination, un-savable, and you can't wait to see me go to hell." But that's not our message. At least it shouldn't be.

One thoughtful way to respond would be to say, "What do you mean by 'homosexuality'?" After reading this book, you now know that the Bible only says that same-sex *sexual behavior* is sin. Same-sex attraction is not a sin, nor is calling yourself gay. The person asking the question is using a really broad term—*homosexuality*—and you can't give a narrow answer to a broad term without being misunderstood.

The topic of homosexuality is far too complex; it defies quick answers. It requires a *conversation*, like the one we're having. Blurting out quick answers will usually shut down any opportunity of having that conversation.

Another way you could respond to the question "What's your view on homosexuality?" is to answer with another question: "Why do you want to know?" This usually gets beneath the surface really quickly and might open up a conversation. Maybe something like this:

"Well, um, because I heard you're a Christian, so I just want to know if you hate gay people."

"Oh, no, I don't hate gay people. Not at all. Why would you think that I hate gay people just because I'm a Christian?"

"Well, my best friend is gay. You see, he grew up in the church. And they teased him like crazy until one day he couldn't take it anymore and he left. He realized he could never love a God who could not love him back, and . . ."

And the conversation begins. You've cut through the question and gotten to the real heart of the matter. And once you do, you'll see that there's a lot of baggage lying beneath the question. Baggage that Jesus would love to carry.

Let me give you one more way you could respond to our question. I got this from my friend Bill Henson, who used to be part of a gay community. He now runs an awesome ministry where he helps Christians reach out to gay people. He's got a great answer, since he's been on both sides of the question. Here's how he responds:

"Bill, do you think homosexuality is a sin?"

Bill's answer: "You know what, that's a really good question. And I would love to talk about it. But can I do something for you? Can I buy you lunch or coffee a couple times a week for the next four weeks? I'd really love to get to know you, and have you get to know me, and then I'd love to talk about your question."

Bill has done this many times, and he says that almost every person takes him up on his offer. He's not avoiding the question. He's going to answer it. But now, his answer will come in the context of a relationship. And once they know how kind and gracious Bill is, his answer will come across with both truth *and* love.

Third, be courageous. Even if you aren't shocked at the sin around you, and even if you give thoughtful answers to "the question," there's a good chance you're still going to face some ridicule. And it's not going to be easy. When people discover your beliefs about the Bible, God, and his will for our sexuality, you're going to be scorned. Some will say you're old-fashioned. Others will say you're unloving. Some will even say you're bigoted. You're going to be mocked, shunned, laughed at, and possibly persecuted. Some of you already have been. And even though you try to be gracious and loving, for some people this will never be enough. But take comfort: Jesus walked the same path. "People shouted at him and made fun of him. But he didn't do the same thing back to them. When he suffered, he didn't say he would make them suffer . . . He left you an example that he expects you to follow" (1 Peter 2:23, 21).

And this may happen even among your fellow Christians. If you are compassionate toward LGBT people, showing them love and affection and grace, some Christians will ridicule you for being soft on sin. They will think you're being too *liberal*. Other Christians, who affirm same-sex relations, may scorn you for holding to outdated beliefs. They will say you're being too *conservative*.

But don't worry about being too liberal or too conservative. Just concern yourself with being too much like Jesus. Lovingly truthful, and truthfully loving.

At some point you should read through Matthew 10. It talks about Jesus sending his twelve apostles into the world and telling them to expect ridicule and persecution. "I am sending you out like sheep among wolves," Jesus tells them. "So be as wise as snakes and as harmless as doves" (Matthew 10:16). The whole chapter is very relevant for our context today. I truly mean it when I say that there's much hardship in store for Christians who believe that same-sex relations are wrong. This view is so quickly becoming outrageous to the world around us. It's inevitable: persecution is coming.

Because of this, our final point is very important. Without it, the first three won't matter.

And that point is, let your love shine brighter than your stance on homosexuality. Persecution is coming, but don't usher it in any sooner by being obnoxious. If I'm going to be mocked and ridiculed, I sure don't want it to be for lack of love.

So love your gay professor. Go out of your way to show him kindness. If he knows you're a Christian, he probably assumes that you hate him. He likely thinks that you believe he's an abomination, that he doesn't deserve the love of Christ. So be different. Shatter his assumptions. Radiate truth and love from your heart. Tell him to come down from that tree so that you can stay at his house.

Is your coworker a lesbian? Target her with grace. Show her the unconditional love of Christ. Don't just tell her, "Jesus loves you." *Show* her that he loves her. Pick up a shift for her if she needs a day off, or give her one of yours if she needs the money. Again, if she knows you're a Christian, it'll blow her mind that you're serving her with tangible acts of grace.

Many LGBT people *expect* us to hate them. But they won't know that Jesus loves them if we don't love them. So be different. Be bold. Let your love permeate and outshine your view on homosexuality.

CHAPTER NINE

CAN I ATTEND A GAY WEDDING . . . AND OTHER QUESTIONS

You probably have many more questions at this point. I know I certainly do! We've already covered some of the main ones that often come up, like how to respond to your friend who comes out as gay. But I'm sure you still have a list of unanswered questions. Practical questions, like "Can I attend a gay wedding?" Ever wonder that? I've wrestled with this one for years.

So here's what we're going to do next in our conversation. I'm going to raise some of the questions that people have asked me over the years, and do my best to answer them. My guess is that you've probably raised some of these same questions as well. Now here's the thing: I'm not sure I can give a black-and-white answer to all of these questions. Some of them aren't directly addressed in Scripture. But what I can do is help us think through some biblical principles that should guide our response to these questions.

So let's continue our conversation by jumping into that first question:

CAN I ATTEND A GAY WEDDING?

I get asked this question more than any other question related to homosexuality. You can probably see why it's tough to answer, but let's lay out the dilemma so that we're all on the same page.

On the one hand, if you refuse to attend the wedding of your gay friend (or family member), this could come off as unloving, self-righteous, and judgmental. Perhaps you're trying to lead your friend to Christ (assuming they're not a Christian already). If you don't attend, they may view this as a denial of the love you say you have for them.

On the other hand, if you attend the wedding, will your friend and others think that you now approve of homosexual relations? Aren't you endorsing gay marriage by attending the wedding?

What do you think? There seems to be a bit of truth in both responses. While I don't think there's a clear right or wrong answer to the question, here are some things to consider.

The first thing to consider is whether the couple claims to be Christian. If they don't, then I don't think it would be a problem to attend their wedding. Remember Paul's words, "What have I to do with judging outsiders?" (1 Corinthians 5:12 ESV). Since we shouldn't expect unbelievers to act like believers, I don't think it would be wrong to attend a gay wedding if they are unbelievers. Or if you refuse to attend, then you should be consistent and not attend any weddings between unbelievers.

But if they do claim to be Christians, then here are a few more things to consider.

Make sure you are consistent in which weddings you attend. If you don't attend the gay wedding, then you also should not attend any Christian wedding that is unbiblical. For instance, marriages between a believer and an unbeliever. Scripture doesn't allow believers to marry unbelievers. Or you shouldn't attend a marriage when one of the partners has been through an unbiblical divorce.

It's pretty hypocritical to attend certain weddings that aren't sanctioned by Scripture yet not attend other weddings that also aren't sanctioned by Scripture.

We also need to ask: What would my attendance communicate to the couple? Will they think that I now approve of their marriage? If so, then I would recommend not going. This would also be hypocritical, if you don't actually affirm their marriage. But if you know the couple getting married, then they probably know that you don't approve of homosexual unions. Your attendance therefore could be interpreted as an act of love toward the person without affirming what they're doing. In this case, I don't think it would be hypocritical for you to attend. Your attendance would only communicate what you're already communicating with your friendship: I don't agree with homosexual behavior—including homosexual marriage—but I still love you.

Now, when people used to attend weddings, their presence meant that they approved of the marriage itself. In fact, ministers used to ask if anyone in the audience disapproved of the wedding. How awkward would that be? You're about to kiss your husband or wife and all of a sudden Uncle Bob stands up and says, "I disapprove of this wedding!" And boom, the wedding's over. Wow! I'm really glad they don't do this anymore. Most weddings today do not give the audience such authority, and people attend a wedding for all sorts of reasons.

So again, you have to ask yourself: What would your presence at the wedding convey to the couple getting married? If it would convey approval of the marriage itself, then you probably shouldn't attend. If it would convey acceptance and love of the person, then I think it might be good to attend.

CAN I ATTEND THE BIRTHDAY PARTY OF MY GAY FRIEND?

This one is pretty easy to answer. Yes, you can attend. Birthday parties don't have the same potential of sending the wrong signals as weddings do. If you attend a wedding, there's a *chance* this could be interpreted as your endorsement of the wedding itself. But the same isn't true of birthday parties, graduations, or other types of celebrations. If you attend a birthday party, all you're saying is, "I'm glad you were born, my friend." And every Christian should be able to say that about all their friends—gay or straight, Christian or Buddhist.

Some people may say, "Yeah, but my gay friend is an unbeliever and her party will have a whole bunch of really bad people there." If this is the case, then I would say you *really* need to attend. Followers of Jesus should be all about hanging out where bad people are hanging out. What better place for a Christian to be than with a group of people who need Jesus the most?

In fact, Jesus was faced with a similar question with his friend Levi (otherwise known as Matthew). Right after Levi became a disciple of Jesus, he threw a massive party to celebrate: "Levi gave a huge banquet for Jesus at his house." And Levi invited all of his friends: "A large crowd of tax collectors and others were eating with them." Naturally, the Pharisees got all upset and complained. "Why do you eat and drink with tax collectors and sinners?" Jesus's response is brilliant. "I have not come to get those who think they are right with God to follow me. I have come to get sinners to turn away from their sins" (Luke 5:27–32).

Jesus came to hang out with people who needed him the most. And so should we. So if your gay friend invites you to her party and you know there's going to be a bunch of tax collectors—I mean, LGBT people or just plain anyone—there who don't know Jesus, then you're not just allowed to go. You *need* to go.

Now, of course, if there's stuff going on at the party that's illegal or going to cause you to sin, then there may be a reason not to go. But this is true of any party or celebration. I mean, going to the mall could also cause you to lust, envy, or believe that you need stuff you don't. This world is a dangerous place, wherever you go. As always, we need to use wisdom and discernment, but also take risks for the sake of the gospel.

With our specific question, however, there's no good reason why you can't attend your gay friend's birthday party or similar celebration.

SHOULD I VOTE FOR A GOVERNOR OR PRESIDENT WHO SUPPORTS GAY MARRIAGE?

Some Christians would never vote for anyone who supports gay marriage. But again, I think we need to be consistent. Do we only vote for candidates who have a perfect Christian standard of right and wrong? Probably not, right? Every candidate is bound to stand for something that goes against our Christian faith. Think about it. Have you ever heard a candidate talk about how we should love our enemies and pray for those who persecute us? But that's what Jesus says we should do (Matthew 5). Or what about greed, divorce, and sex outside of marriage. Does any candidate ever stand against these?

The fact is, every candidate is probably going to promote some biblical values while standing against others. The question is, which of those values are more important? Is gay marriage at the top of that list? Will gay marriages hinder God's kingdom from advancing? Probably not. While I don't agree that same-sex marriages are within God's will, I don't think it would be wrong to vote for someone who supports gay marriage.

We should also consider a related question: *Should we vote for or against laws that legalize gay marriage?* It's hard to predict the future, but I imagine that there will be some attempts to overturn the Supreme Court's June 2015 decision to legalize gay marriage. Should we vote for or against potential attempts to overturn the Court's decision? This one's a bit different. It's one thing to vote for a candidate who stands for a lot of great things and yet happens to support gay marriage. But to vote directly in support of the legalization of gay marriage? I don't think I could do this. Voting for gay marriage would go directly against my convictions about what marriage is and what the Bible says about same-sex relations. How could I vote for it?

I know several Christians who stand against gay marriage in the church, yet believe that we should allow for the state to recognize same-sex marriages. I still lean toward voting in line with your convictions—voting for traditional marriage—but I can see how the separation of church and state could lead a Christian to vote for gay marriage. Either way, I don't think that Christians should focus on secular politics but on Christian ethics; our energy should be directed toward what the Bible says about homosexuality and how we can best love those who experience same-sex attraction. The secular nations will act—and vote—like the nations.

WHAT ABOUT "GAY CHRISTIANS"?

Okay, now this is a really tough question. For most of our conversation, we've been talking about LGBT people who aren't professing Christians. But what about LGBT people who claim to know and follow Christ? Can they really be Christians? Are they actually gay?

To answer these questions, we first have to specify what we mean by "gay" or "LGBT." Remember, the Bible only forbids homosexual sex and not same-sex attraction. If by "gay" we simply mean someone who's attracted to the same sex but doesn't believe it's right to act on it, then yes, of course they can be Christian. Likewise, if someone is transgender and feels more like the opposite sex, this isn't necessarily sin. I do think that getting a sex change is sin, since it fundamentally alters one's God-given body. Or if someone doesn't get a sex change but lives out their identity in ways contrary to their biological sex, this could be sin as well. But as you can imagine, there's a bit of a gray area here. What if a woman cuts her hair short and wears baggy blue jeans? Is this sin? Not necessarily. It's not about the fabric of clothes or the length of hair; it's all about the heart. The main question is this: Are you seeking to live out your God-given gender in a way that reflects your biological sex? Struggling with gender identity is not a sin. Acting on that struggle might be.

But what about Christians who don't agree with what I've said about the Bible in our conversation? These Christians have read the same verses, yet think that the Bible doesn't forbid consensual same-sex relations. Two people of the same sex can get married, have sex, and adopt children. Can someone hold such a view and be Christian?

The real question comes when someone is engaging in the sin of homosexual sex *and believes that such an act is perfectly fine* and yet continues to confess Christ. The Bible considers this to be sexual immorality. And there's a good chance that those who persist in sexual immorality are not genuinely saved. But at the end of the day, only God knows.

Maybe they are genuinely saved and only backsliding. Or maybe they aren't truly saved. It's hard for us humans to know for sure.

It's important to remember the words of Jesus:

"You look at the bit of sawdust in your friend's eye. But you pay no attention to the piece of wood in your own eye. How can you say to your friend, 'Let me take the bit of sawdust out of your eye'? How can you say this while there is a piece of wood in your own eye?" (Matthew 7:3–4)

We need to make sure we're focusing more on our own sin than on the sin of others. If we're engaging in heterosexual sexual sin (pornography, lust, sex), then who are we to judge those engaging in homosexual sin? We should first deal with our own sin before we help others get out of their sin.

CAN GAY PEOPLE CHANGE THEIR SEXUAL ORIENTATION?

This question has been answered very differently over the years. Some people have said, "Yes! Gay people can change," while others have said, "No, they can't! And it's dangerous to tell them they can."

So what's the answer?

The best answer is that it's possible for gay people to change their orientation, but it's very unlikely. At least, it's unlikely that they will experience a full-blown change from gay to straight. I've heard some stories about people who have experienced such a change, so I don't want to say it can't happen. After all, nothing is impossible with God. But I've heard many more stories about people who have tried to change, or been told by others that they can change, and yet experienced little to no change at all. And I know many gay people who have been very discouraged about not experiencing the change they expected. Or they've been convinced that they really have become straight, even though deep down they actually haven't.

A few years ago, a couple psychologists surveyed some people with same-sex attraction who tried to change their orientation. In this study, 15 percent said they experienced a significant degree of change, and 23 percent said they experienced some degree of change. The rest experienced little to no change at all.[1] So some change is possible. But radical change is very unlikely.

There are two things I've learned about the whole "can gay people change" debate. First, if a same-sex-attracted person is going to try to change, *they* must be the one who desires it. It shouldn't be forced upon them by their parents, friends, or pastor. Second, the person seeking change should have realistic expectations. They shouldn't assume that if they try to change it will work. And they shouldn't think that if they are truly seeking God then he will take away their same-sex desires. For whatever reason, God has not taken away same-sex desires from many people who have pursued him with all their heart. And third, we shouldn't equate

1   Mark A. Yarhouse, *Homosexuality: The Use of Scientific Research in the Church's Moral Debate* (Downers Grove, IL: InterVarsity Press, 2000), page 88.

"being straight" with "being holy." Remember, same-sex *attraction* isn't a sin; only same-sex lust and behavior are sin. The good news of the gospel isn't that Jesus came to make gay people straight, but that he came to forgive us of all of our sins and make us all holy.

ARE GAY PEOPLE FORBIDDEN FROM GETTING MARRIED?

The Bible only says that people of the same sex should not have sex. Therefore, it's implied that two people of the same sex shouldn't get married. I actually know of a few people who are married to partners of the same sex and yet they don't engage in sexual relations because they believe that it's sin. But these cases are extremely rare and probably wouldn't work for most people.

So what are the options for Christians who are attracted to the same sex?

Let me just talk directly to those of you who are attracted to the same sex. The rest of you can listen in.

We've already talked about the pros and cons of trying to change your sexual orientation. So you'll need to consider that option with care and much counsel. But if you don't try to go this route, there are a couple other options.

First, you could still marry a person of the opposite sex. This is called a "mixed orientation (or MO) marriage," since one partner is straight while the other partner is gay. This may not sound thrilling to you, and I get that. I truly do.

You probably feel the same about marrying an opposite-sex partner as I would feel about marrying a same-sex partner! So I can understand how you feel. But let me at least say that I've known a few gay people who are in an MO marriage and it's actually worked out much better than you might expect. Their relationships first began as a really solid friendship. But over time, the gay partner began to feel a deeper attraction to their friend, and vice versa. They ended up getting married and having kids, and although they have some very unique struggles (as you could imagine), they have experienced a life-giving marriage.

Now, let me warn you. There are many other people who have tried this and it hasn't worked out well. There are many MO marriages that end in divorce, pain, and confusion. So I don't want to make it sound all peaches and cream. But it is an option.

If an MO marriage is going to work, the couple absolutely *must* be completely honest with each other up front and throughout their relationship. They must talk about their attractions, their struggles, their fears and expectations. If they don't communicate, it simply won't work. In fact, two of my gay friends who are in MO marriages believe that if the couple isn't radically transparent from the very beginning, the marriage will be a disaster. It's also important that you don't feel outside pressure from friends or family to pursue an MO marriage. Again, if you pursue such a marriage because other people want you to, it'll likely be a catastrophic failure.

If you are considering an MO marriage as an option for the future, then I would highly recommend having a few people deeply involved in your relationship. Perhaps an older couple, or another believer who is attracted to the same sex. Mixed orientation marriages are bound to fail if the partners don't invite others into their lives.

Now, if you can't (or don't try to) change your orientation, and you don't pursue a mixed orientation marriage, then there's always the option of celibacy. You might think that you'd rather roll around naked in a room full of broken glass than to be celibate your whole life, but hear me out.

Being celibate does *not* mean you have to be lonely. I know a lot of married people who are terribly lonely. Just look at how many Christians have affairs! Marriage won't automatically solve your loneliness. I know some really lonely celibate people, but I also know some who are relationally fulfilled. How do they experience this?

Community.

Humans can live without sex. But we can't live without love. We can't live without relationships and community. And we can have rich, vibrant, life-giving relationships without having sex with those we're in relationship with. I think our society has elevated sex way too much and has equated sex with love. But love is not the same as sex, and sex is not the same as love. Don't get me wrong. Sex is pretty awesome. But I've experienced love and relational fulfillment apart from marriage and sex.

The celibate gay people I know who are living fulfilled lives are surrounded by an authentic body of believers who treat each other like family. There's no doubt about it—going without sex is tough! And again, I don't want to say it'll be easy. But life will bring many difficulties your way. Life is filled with trials and pain and happy times and lonely times. Living a life of celibacy will have its own struggles. But if you keep Jesus at the center of your life, and dive into a community of believers who are committed to you, then you could live an exhilarating, joy-filled life.

I love Paul's words in 2 Corinthians 4:

> Our troubles are small. They last only for a short time. But they are earning for us a glory that will last forever. It is greater than all our troubles. So we don't spend all our time looking at what we can see. Instead, we look at what we can't see. That's because what can be seen lasts only a short time. But what can't be seen will last forever. (2 Corinthians 4:17–18)

And remember: Paul was single. He wasn't gay, but he gets the celibate life. It's a life filled with both trials and joy, loneliness and relational fulfillment. And at the end of the day, all of our hardship in this life will pass away and we will enter into the bliss of eternal life with God.

We could stay up all night tackling more questions, but why don't we end here. The few that we talked about should give you a feel for how we can display both truth and love when it comes to the real-life implications of homosexuality in our world. I think it's important to keep in mind that we're all on a journey and we need to be okay with failure. I mean, don't strive for failure! But the fact is, we're all going to do stupid things and say things that are offensive. I can't tell you how many times I've looked back on a conversation I had or a blog I wrote and thought, "I can't believe I said that!" Sometimes we'll err on the side of truth and other times we'll err on the side of love. The key is to keep learning, keep trying, keep following Jesus down this strange and adventurous road we call life.

CONCLUSION

As we wrap up our conversation, I want to summarize a few of the major points we've talked about. I know some of you still have questions about what the Bible says about homosexuality, and you want to stay after and chat some more. I'm totally willing to do this. We'll call our chat "Appendix."

For the rest of you who have to go, let's sum up the main things we've learned in this book.

Homosexuality is about people. Hopefully, by now you have a much broader view of homosexuality and LGBT people. Both society and the church have tended to stereotype LGBT people and treat homosexuality in a simplistic manner. Many Christians just want to know, "Is it a sin?" without even knowing what "it" is or realizing that there are many other important questions to ask. Homosexuality is a bundle of diverse questions and issues and topics and problems. Most of all, it's a bundle of diverse *people*. Even if you forget some of the points in our discussion, always remember: Homosexuality is about *people*.

Throughout our discussion, you've heard many stories of LGBT people. And my hope is that these stories help you never to treat homosexuality as just some issue. I would encourage you to find your own stories. Go out and meet some LGBT people. Ask them questions. Listen to their stories. Enter their joy and their pain. You'll quickly see that there is much more about these individuals than just a desire for same-sex relations.

My lesbian friend Julie Rogers says, "Over the course of the 10,080 minutes that go by in a given week, very few of those minutes (if any at all) are likely comprised of sexual thoughts about other women." Unfortunately, many Christians have reduced people like Julie to those few minutes—just another lesbian who desires sex with other women. But that's a terribly inaccurate picture of who Julie is.

So go! Love, learn, and listen. Don't just sit around and talk about gay people with all of your straight friends. Follow Jesus—he just might be on his way to hang out with some gay friends.

Believe the Bible. Early on in our discussion, we dove into the Scriptures to see what they say about marriage and same-sex relations. And if you want even more biblical depth, then please stick around for our "Appendix" chat.

What we've seen is that the Bible says that same-sex relations are not within the will of God. We've seen this from several angles:

- The Bible only endorses male and female marriages.

- The Bible sometimes even highlights male and female differences within marriage.

- The Old Testament explicitly forbids homosexual sexual intercourse.

- The New Testament also explicitly forbids both male and female same-sex intercourse.

- Jesus's silence about homosexuality can't be taken as indifference or affirmation.

The Bible, therefore, says that same-sex sexual relations are a sin. However, we can't stop here. We can't just say "The Bible says it's a sin" and stop there. We also must imitate the way in which Jesus loved and accepted all types of people. We need to be full of love and full of truth—truthfully loving and lovingly truthful.

Therefore, to be truly Jesus-like and biblical means that we should:

- Stop saying and doing things that make LGBT people feel less than human. No more gay jokes. No more looks of disgust and contempt. No more destructive words like "fag," "homo," "abomination," or any other word that communicates hate rather than love.

- Be exceedingly welcoming to LGBT people in our churches and Christian communities. "Welcoming" doesn't mean affirming everyone's behavior, but it does mean accepting a person's humanity. People can't obey God until they first know they are accepted by God—and by God's people.

- Believe that we all are sinful before God and in need

of his grace. All of the passages that mention same-sex sin also list many sins that straight people commit every day. Being biblical means not being a hypocrite.

- Not just tell LGBT people that God loves them. We need to *show* them that God loves them *by* loving them ourselves.

If you're standing for truth and yet failing to love, then you're not standing for truth at all. Remember, the marginalized, sinners, tax collectors, and outcasts all loved being around Jesus. Do those who feel like outcasts in our religious circles today love being around you?

Listen, learn, love. We kept coming back to this point throughout our conversation. Many Christians need to be better listeners. To listen is to love, and you can't love without listening. Too often, we voice our opinions and beliefs, yet we don't genuinely consider the stories and views and pains and struggles of other people—especially those with a very different set of struggles than ours.

But listening in love doesn't mean you agree with everything you hear. Just because you listen to a girl share about the love she felt for another girl doesn't mean you think that lesbian relations are okay. Just because you learn about another boy's same-sex attraction doesn't mean you think he should act on it.

So don't be afraid to dive into somebody's life by hearing their story. You might find yourself identifying with Jesus, who took the time to enter our sin and shame, who sat on the edge of a well and chatted with a Samaritan woman who was living with a man who was not her husband. Or dined in the home of a traitor named Zacchaeus, while all the religious people grumbled outside. Or showed up at Levi's wild party that was stuffed with immoral people.

Being a Christian is a dangerous thing. You might find yourself loved by "unlovable" people and hated by your friends; at home with the homeless and cast out by the religious elite. But at the end of the day, we will all stand before Jesus, and he won't ask for your church attendance or a memory verse. He won't want to see a list of how many people you witnessed to, or how many times you refused to drink a beer. He won't wonder if you've led a Bible study or gone on a mission trip. And he won't show you a record of how many hours of Netflix you watched.

He will ask whether you loved (Matthew 25:31–46).

APPENDIX: DOES THE BIBLE REALLY SAY iT'S WRONG?

INTRODUCTION

Earlier in our conversation, we talked about what the Bible says about marriage and homosexual relations. Maybe you thought our conversation was pretty heavy. Or maybe you thought our conversation was not heavy enough! Either way, the discussion of what the Bible says about homosexuality goes much deeper than what we were able to cover in our conversation so far. So I want to take time here to address some of the most powerful and popular arguments that people give in support of same-sex relations. Maybe you've heard some of these arguments already; they're becoming fairly well known. Anyway, I want to respond to five of the strongest arguments in favor of same-sex relations. Let me give you a quick word of warning: If you want even more depth, then check out my other book, *People to Be Loved*. There, I go into even greater detail on what the Bible says about homosexuality.

ARGUMENT 1: THE TYPE OF HOMOSEXUALITY IN BIBLE TIMES IS NOT THE SAME AS TODAY

This argument goes like this: *It's true that the Bible prohibits same-sex relations, but the only types of homosexual relations that existed back then were oppressive and exploitative. There was no such thing as mutual, consensual, monogamous, same-sex relations.*

This is actually a convincing argument. After all, the Bible can't condemn something that didn't exist. So if mutual, same-sex relations didn't exist back then, then the Bible must be talking about something else. And it is true that *most* same-sex relations in the ancient world were *not* consensual, mutual, or monogamous. They were relationships between a man and a boy, a man and his male slave, or a man and a male prostitute. If you look at ancient history, very rarely do we see two consenting adults of the same sex hook up and fall in love.

The argument, however, is not quite accurate for at least three reasons. First, while *most* same-sex relations weren't consensual, some were. This is true especially in ancient Greek culture. There are quite a few examples of two consenting men having an ongoing relationship with each other. For instance, there was a famous Greek poet named Agathon, who dressed like a woman and had a lifelong, consensual lover named Pausanias.[1]

---

1   Plato, *Symposium* 193B; cf. Aelian, *Varia historia* 2.21; Aristophophanes, *Thesmophoria Women*, 1-276; See ibid. 142-143.

Such consensual relationships were less popular during the Roman times (when the New Testament was written), but they still existed. For instance, a first-century Jewish writer named Josephus says, "What are our laws about marriage? The law owns no other mixture of sexes but that which according to nature."[2] Notice that Josephus is not talking about rape, prostitution, or men having sex with boys. He's talking about *marriage* between two people of the same sex. Likewise, a famous second-century (AD) writer named Ptolemy of Alexandria refers to women taking other women as "lawful wives."[3]

So it's true that *most* same-sex relations were not consensual. But to say that they didn't exist is just plain wrong.

Second, while same-sex relations among *men* were usually exploitative, the same is not true of *female* same-sex relations. This is actually a really important point that many people miss. Female same-sex relations *were* most often consensual and mutual. And yet the Bible says they are wrong: "God let them continue to have their shameful desires. Their women committed sexual acts that were not natural" (Romans 1:26). Since female same-sex relations were most often consensual, and since Romans 1 doesn't specify nonconsensual relations, it's almost impossible that Romans 1 is only prohibiting nonconsensual relations.

A third reason the Bible isn't just talking about nonconsensual same-sex relations is because of the language of mutuality. We've already talked about this earlier, but it's important to highlight the point again. When Leviticus prohibits same-sex intercourse, it says:

---

2   Josephus, *Ag. Apion* 2.199.

3   Ptolemy of Alexandria, *Tetrabiblos* 3.14 sec. 172; Brooten, *Love Between Women*, 332.

"Suppose a man has sex with another man as he would have sex with a woman. I hate what *they have done. They* must be put to death. Anything that happens to *them* will be *their* own fault." (Leviticus 20:13, emphasis added)

Romans 1 also says:

Their women committed sexual acts that were not natural. In the same way, the men turned away from their natural love for women. They burned with sexual desire for *each other.* Men did shameful things with other men. They suffered in their bodies for all the wrong things *they did.* (verses 26–27, emphasis added)

Notice all the "theys" and "theirs" and "thems." These passages don't talk about one person violating another person; there's no mention of men having sex with boys, or prostitutes, or slaves. Rather, the passages talk about mutual acts between consenting adults. Both passages talk about mutual guilt.

Again, it's true that *most* (male) same-sex relationships in the ancient world were not consensual. But if you consider all three of the points above, it's clear that the Bible prohibits *all types* of same-sex relations and not just certain ones.

ARGUMENT 2: ROMANS 1 PROHIBITS EXCESSIVE LUST, NOT MUTUAL SAME-SEX LOVE

Let's look at the first of two arguments often raised with regard to Romans 1. The first one says that Romans 1 is actually targeting same-sex relations that are driven by *excessive lust* and *that's why* they are condemned.

If you look closely at the context, you can see why people say this. Some English translations use the term "lust" throughout Romans 1:24–27 (NIV, NLT). The Greek words being used, though, simply refer to "passion," or in this context "sexual passion." The passage isn't really saying that these relationships were wrong *because* they were lustful—as if non-lustful same-sex relations would be perfectly fine. Obviously when two people have sex, there's probably a lot of burning passion involved. That's all Paul is saying here. He's describing a mutual sex act between two people of the same sex, and he condemns it because they're of the same sex.

Plus, the three points I raised in the first argument apply to this one as well: (1) evidence of some consensual relations among males, (2) consensual relations among females, and (3) the language of mutuality. Therefore, it's very unlikely that Paul was only saying that same-sex relations that are driven by lust are wrong, while non-lustful relations are perfectly fine.

ARGUMENT 3: ROMANS 1 REFERS TO IDOLATROUS SEX, NOT CONSENSUAL SAME-SEX RELATIONS

This argument is similar to the previous one. Some say that Paul is not condemning all types of same-sex relations, but only certain types of relations: specifically, ones that were connected with idolatry. After all, Paul specifically mentions idolatry earlier on in Romans 1:23: "They would rather have statues of gods than the glorious God who lives forever. Their statues of gods are made to look like people, birds, animals and reptiles."

There's no denying that the larger context of Romans 1 is idolatry. However, Paul is not saying that same-sex relations *that are connected with idolatry* are wrong while other same-sex relations are totally fine. Read Romans 1:18–32 carefully. Paul says that we're all committing idolatry when we choose sin over serving our Creator. That's what idolatry is. Paul is not just talking about literally bowing down to statues—although this is certainly included. He's talking about serving and honoring and desiring other things in the place of God. All sin is idolatry.

Let's look at it from another angle. Paul doesn't just single out same-sex relations in the chapter. Remember, there are a lot of different sins listed at the end of the chapter; just read Romans 1:24–32. Does this mean that Paul only condemns *idolatrous forms of murder, lying, pride, cheating, and hating* (Romans 1:29–30)? I don't think so. I'm pretty sure Paul thinks that all murder is wrong. All pride is wrong. All cheating is wrong. I don't think Paul is condemning certain idolatrous forms of cheating while applauding non-idolatrous forms of cheating.

Paul also doesn't single out certain types of sins that are connected with idolatry. Rather, he's saying that all sin is the result of turning from our Creator and serving the creation. All sin, therefore, *is* idolatry.

ARGUMENT 4: 1 CORINTHIANS 6 IS TALKING ABOUT EXPLOITATIVE SEX, NOT CONSENSUAL RELATIONS

You can probably see a pattern by now. Most of the arguments against a traditional view say that the Bible isn't talking about consensual relations. But we've seen several problems with these arguments.

In any case, some people apply the "lack of consensuality" argument to 1 Corinthians 6, where Paul says, "Those who commit sexual sins will not receive the kingdom . . . *Neither will men who sleep with other men*" (verse 9, emphasis added). You may wonder how some people could say that this verse is not talking about consensual relations. After all, it just says "men who sleep with other men."

This verse is actually much more complicated than it seems. To understand the complexity, we have to talk about the two original Greek words that Paul uses here.

The English phrase "men who sleep with other men" is a translation of two Greek words: *malakoi*, which means "soft," and *arsenokoites*, which probably means "men who sleep with males," although Greek scholars disagree on its meaning. *Malakoi* is only used a few times in the New Testament and *arsenokoites* is only used once—here in 1 Corinthians 6. When words are rare, it's sometimes difficult to know what they mean. This is true of any language, even English. For instance, you've probably never heard the word *ailurophilia*, even if you're fluent in English. Just because you understand a language well doesn't mean you know the meaning of every rare word. Now, with the help of Google, you can find out in two seconds that *ailurophilia* simply means "the love of cats," but it's a lot harder to find out the precise meaning of rare Greek words.

Lucky for us, though *malakoi* isn't used too often in the New Testament, it was widely used in other pieces of literature around Paul's time. So this word is pretty easy to figure out. Basically, the word literally means "soft," but it was often used to describe men who looked and acted like women. Such men were called "soft," which basically means "effeminate" or "womanly." In many contexts, the word was used to describe effeminate men who had sex with other men. (Or, without getting too graphic, men *had sex* with *them*.)

This is probably what *malakoi* means here. Effeminate men who gave themselves to other men sexually.

Figuring out the meaning of *arsenokoites* is much more difficult. Not only is this the first and only time it's used in the New Testament, this is the *first time it's ever used in Greek literature as a whole*. Paul probably invented the word, which makes it tough to define.

Tough—but not impossible. Here's why.

Arsenokoites is a compound word from *arsen* and *koites*. *Arsen* means "male" and *koites* literally means "bed," but is often used of sexual relations (like our English word *coitus*). So the word literally means "men who sleep with other males."

But some people say that you can't figure out a word just by looking at its compound parts. After all, the word "butterfly" has nothing to do with lathering up an insect with that golden goodness (I'm a big fan of butter!). So maybe *arsenokoites* means "men who sleep with males" or maybe it means something different. We need more evidence to determine the meaning.

Such evidence is found in Leviticus. Here's what's interesting: Even though the word *arsenokoites* was never used prior to Paul, the compound parts *arsen* and *koite* were. In fact, these two words are used in Leviticus 20:13—the verse that forbids men from sleeping with other males.[4]

Let's pull our discussion together. *Arsenokoites* was a word created by Paul by reading Leviticus 20:13 and drawing on its prohibition of male homosexual sex. The word, therefore, does in fact mean "men who sleep with males." And *malakoi* often refers to men who are, so to speak, *slept with*. Together, these words are rightly interpreted as "men who give themselves for sex with other men" and "the men who sleep with those men." If Paul meant to single out exploitative sex—men sleeping with boys or male prostitutes—he doesn't clearly say so. Rather, Paul uses words that just refer to men having sex with males, not a certain type of male nor a certain type of sex act.

ARGUMENT 5: THE BIBLICAL WRITERS DIDN'T KNOW ABOUT SEXUAL ORIENTATION

Another powerful argument against the traditional view is that the concept of same-sex *orientation* wasn't around back

---

4   To be specific, the two Greek words *arsen* and *koite* are used in the Greek translation of the Hebrew Old Testament. This Greek version (called the "Septuagint") was translated around 100 BC and was the primary version of the Old Testament used by the writers of the New Testament, including Paul.

then. We now know that some people are born with a fixed attraction to the same sex. It's not their fault: It's the way they were born. They can't change. And they aren't supposed to change since God made them that way.

We talked about a similar argument way back at the beginning of our discussion. Remember that? Some people say that since people are born with same-sex attraction, it therefore must be okay to act on that attraction. But there are all sorts of problems with this logic. The Bible never says that one's desire for a certain act or behavior automatically justifies the act. In fact, the Bible frequently says that our desires and feelings are just as messed up as our intellect, will, and behaviors. The whole "born with it" argument is not a good biblical argument.

Plus, as we have seen, the causes of same-sex orientation are very complex. It's scientifically naïve to say that everyone who feels attracted to the same sex was born with a same-sex orientation. All of the best studies show that both nature and nurture play complex roles in forming same-sex desires.

In any case, let's just say that everyone who's attracted to the same sex is born with a fixed same-sex orientation. Would this change the biblical commands?

I don't think it would. In fact, the idea that some people are born with a fixed sexual orientation was around in the first century. I don't know how widespread it was, and I don't know if the biblical writers were aware of this view. But I have found about a dozen different references in ancient literature, where some people were believed to have a fixed same-sex desire from birth. One scholar who has looked at these sources says, "Contrary to the view that the idea of sexual orientation did not develop until the nineteenth century, the astrological sources demonstrate the existence in the Roman world of the concept of a lifelong erotic orientation."[5] And this scholar is a lesbian. She's not just trying to support some conservative view of the Bible. Quite the opposite, actually.

Maybe the biblical writers were aware of same-sex orientation, or maybe they weren't. We can't say for sure. What we can say is that the concept of sexual orientation wasn't unknown in the first century.

But even if it was unknown, I still don't think this would matter. The Bible says that particular acts are wrong—including same-sex intercourse. Just because we now have a greater understanding of the desires that may lead to that act, that doesn't change the biblical stance on the act. Remember, we are born into a fallen world and we possess fallen emotions, bodies, and desires. Even our sexual orientation is subject to sin.

---

5   Bernadette Brooten, *Love Between Women*, 140.

For additional content and videos visit

LivingInAGrayWorld.com

Connect with the author!

PrestonSprinkle.com
 /@PrestonSprinkle

People to Be Loved

Why Homosexuality Is Not Just an Issue

Preston Sprinkle

Christians who are confused by the homosexuality debate raging in the U.S. are looking for resources that are based solidly on a deep study of what Scripture says about the issue. In *People to Be Loved*, Preston Sprinkle challenges those on all sides of the debate to consider what the Bible says and how we should approach the topic of homosexuality in light of it.

In a manner that appeals to a scholarly and lay-audience alike, Preston takes on difficult questions such as how should the church treat people struggling with same-sex attraction? Is same-sex attraction a product of biological or societal factors or both? How should the church think about larger cultural issues, such as gay marriage, gay pride, and whether intolerance over LGBT amounts to racism? How (or if) Christians should do business with LGBT persons and supportive companies?

Simply saying that the Bible condemns homosexuality is not accurate, nor is it enough to end the debate. Those holding a traditional view still struggle to reconcile the Bible's prohibition of same-sex attraction with the message of radical, unconditional grace. This book meets that need.

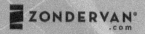